The Farm Kid
And
The Flying Bank

An Autobiography

By

Dennis Gordon McConnell

Copyrights ©2026 by Dennis McConnell

All Rights Reserved.

DEDICATION

This book is dedicated to my children, Jean, Lory, and Jill, with special thanks to my sister, Val, who reviewed the manuscript and pointed out necessary corrections. I also wish to acknowledge my curling friend, Henry Tersen, whose encouragement gave me the confidence to see this story through to publication. Finally, I thank my great-granddaughter, Jada Nordin, for the wonderful job she did designing the book cover.

TABLE OF CONTENTS

Note: This book was first written for the author's children. "Connecting the Dots" was originally a chapter to explain their place in the family but was later moved to the appendix. Many names appear in both the book and appendix, so readers can refer to it for clarity about who the author mentions.

1

WHERE IT STARTED...

I was born in the Peace River, Alberta Hospital June 12, 1941, to Robert Gordon McConnell (DOB July 30, 1911) and Grace Yvonne McConnell (nee Brown) (DOB June 30, 1924).

For a brief history of Mom and Dad, I am inserting their stories, as published in the Nampa History Book, which was printed in about 1980, at the end of *my* story. You might want to read those first; they did come before me.

Mom & Dad were married Oct. 3, 1940, and I arrived in June 1941.

My sister Val (Eva Valerie) was born Feb. 3, 1943, and then Lynne (Heather Lynne) was born June 2, 1945. Mom lost two babies in about 1947 and 1949, and baby brother Gavin Clifford was born on March 9, 1951.

Lynne passed away in July 2020 at age 75 during the COVID pandemic due to a blood disease, which was exacerbated by an infectious disease known as "C. Difficile."[1]

---

[1] (Clostridioides difficile (klos-TRID-e-oi-deez dif-uh-SEEL) is a bacterium that causes an infection of the colon, the longest part of the large intestine. Symptoms can range from diarrhea to life-threatening damage to the colon. The bacterium is often called C. difficile or C. diff.

Illness from C. difficile often occurs after using antibiotic medicines. It mostly affects older adults in hospitals or in long-term care settings. People not in care settings or hospitals can also get C. difficile infection. Some strains of the bacterium that can cause serious infections are more likely to affect younger people.

The bacterium used to be called Clostridium (klos-TRID-e-um) difficile.)

The Farm Kid and The Flying Bank

Mom, Dad, Val & Dennis fall of 1943. I like Mom's Mickey Mouse ears.

Dennis, Val, Lynne & Lassie (about 1946) at "Cliff's" place. The "old garage" in the background with Cliff's car (a "Terraplane")[2]

My first home was at what my folks referred to as "The Mott Place" (NW ¼ of 2-82-20), about 8

---

[2] It took guts to launch a new model line in the midst of the Great Depression, but Hudson managed to pull it off with the stylish and popular Terraplane of 1932 through 1938. The Hudson Motor Car Company of Detroit (1910-1957) was a well-respected maker of upper-middle-priced cars in the Buick-Olds range that, due to the limited sales potential in that category, reached down into the low-priced range periodically to fill out its production capacity. Low-priced brands in the Hudson family of cars included the successful Essex of 1919-32, the unsuccessful Hudson Jet of 1953-54, and maybe the most memorable of the bunch, the popular Terraplane of 1932 through 1938.

miles northeast of Nampa, Alberta. I recall Mom and Dad mentioning several times that it was a mouse-infested old shack. When I was about 6 months old, we moved to what was my Grandma McConnell's house on the NW¼ of 3-80-20 -about 6 miles NE of Nampa. My Grandma McConnell bought this quarter for $300 after my Grandpa Jack McConnell died in 1934. A comfortable log house was built for my Grandma, along with my Dad and his siblings, who were still at home. Dad's brothers, Alex and Cliff, had enlisted in WWII, and, as the eldest, Dad was permitted to stay home to look after the farm.

Around 1941, the family built a small house in the village of Nampa for my Grandma. When she died in about 1943, the farm was left to my Uncle Cliff. In 2001, the house was still standing (see photo). When Cliff joined the army, my Dad managed the farm until Cliff's return in 1945. In July of 1945, my Dad bought his first quarter (SE ¼ of 5-82-20) from Olie Gronlund.

We continued to live in the log house (which was now Uncle Cliff's) for a few years and, as near as I can remember, Cliff, who never married, lived with us for a while when he first returned from overseas.

In 1947, we moved to an old house on the Gronlund land until Dad was able to build a new home in 1948. Our quarter was located two miles North of Nampa, and 1 ¾ miles east on the "McKinnon Highway," which is now known as the "South Harmon Valley Road."

Cliff's house...photo taken in 2001

I remember starting school while we lived at Uncle Cliff's, where I was picked up at the gate by a Van type School bus driven by John Bambush, who lived about a half mile past our place. He had to open the back doors of the van, and we climbed in where we sat on wooden benches along each side for the 6-mile ride to Nampa. The only resemblance it had to today's school buses was that it was yellow.

The Farm Kid and The Flying Bank

I was still in Grade 1 when we moved to the old Gronlund house and had just turned seven and was ready for Grade two when we moved into our new house in the summer of 1948. I had to walk to what was known as the Trowsdale corner to catch the same bus—about ½ mile walk from the Gronlund place and only about ¼ mile walk from our new house.

In the winter, it was dark when I left home for the walk to the bus, and I was scared to death that the coyotes would get me, but they never did.

By the time Val started school in 1949, I had company for the walk, and the fear of coyotes diminished. I figured I could outrun her if the coyotes showed up. I asked Val how we got to school that year because I couldn't remember.

It turns out that was the year we were sent to school in Peace River while the new school in Nampa was being built—so there goes my coyote story. Here's the help I got from Val.

Dear forgetful one,

John Bambush picked us up at the gate in an old panel truck. Kathleen Bambush and Ethel Mayowski got to sit up front. The rest of us sat on wooden benches along the sides of the bus. There were, as I recall, old gray army blankets to put over us to keep us warm. I do remember being so tired after a long day in grade one that I would sometimes doze off leaning on Doug Sherris. You were at Riverside School in Peace River for that year, but I went there until Christmas and then, for some reason, all the Nampa kids in Grade 1 were switched to Centre Street.

I can't recall exactly everyone on that bus, but I remember Georgie Bambush and Nat Barnowski, Mel and Doug Sherris, and Phyllis Sherris, too, I think (Shorty's daughter who lived with Lottie and Logan that year).

Anything else?

I can remember riding in the panel bus with a couple of Indigenous kids, a girl about my age, I think, whose last name was "Ghostkeeper." There was also an indigenous kid whose last name was Amato. I remember him because he used to chew gum, and as he couldn't chew gum in class, he would store it behind his ear.

2
FOND CHILDHOOD MEMORIES

Some of my earliest and *mostly* fondest memories include these:

I remember Mom coming home from the hospital with Baby Lynne. I remember pulling up a chair to stand on so I could get a better look at her while Mom held her in her arms.

I remember Aunt Millie—Uncle Alex's English war bride—and Cousin Ian arriving from England in 1946. They had arrived by train from Halifax, where they had disembarked from their journey by ship. I guess I was about four and a half, and Ian wasn't quite three. I remember helping to take off his winter clothes, and I remember referring to him as a little punk, which horrified Aunt Millie— apparently, "punk" to them was slang for a penis.

Aunt Millie had brought along several pairs of clogs—an English shoe with wooden bottoms and leather uppers—for most of her Canadian nieces and nephews living in the Nampa area, and we had at least one of them kicking around our house for years. I don't recall ever actually wearing them other than occasionally around the house. I don't think they were comfortable.

I remember springtime at Uncle Cliff's place. There was always a field of buttercups between the house and the dugout, a couple of hundred yards away. In fact, when I think of my early childhood, that field of buttercups is the first thing that pops into my mind.

I remember our old dog, Lassie, a border Collie, who was a fine dog. Later, we had a male dog called Laddie, but I can't remember how they left this world or when.

I remember a big colourful moth on one of the bedroom windows while we were living at Cliff's. I think I was about four and Val about two.

Anyway, I wanted to capture this beautiful thing—I always liked bugs—and found an old pick handle to hit it with. I'm not sure if it lived or died, but I know the window didn't survive. I ran and dragged Val along, and we hid in a wagon box.

Of course, the crash brought Mom on the run, and she kept calling for us. I can't remember if she found us or if we gave up hiding, but I don't think I got a spanking.

I remember riding with Dad on our old seed drill being pulled by four horses. The old drill had a wooden platform all along the back of it for the precise purpose of standing while riding or driving the team. I would be no more than four or five at that time, as it wasn't long after that that Dad began using a tractor to pull the seeder, the same old seeder for several years.

This isn't Dad's seed drill, but one just like it.

I remember Dad needing to bend—or straighten—a big bolt so he got it red hot in the blacksmith forge in an old garage we had at Cliff's place. He asked me to hold it with pliers as he hammered on it.

With the first blow, it went flying and caught me between the eyes. I bled a lot! I was only five or six at the time, and I believe I still have a bit of a scar there. What I remember most about the affair is the chewing out that Dad got from Mom for expecting a little kid to hold the bolt.

I remember getting dumped by Chile, our pony, into the slough when I was about five. We had this big slough behind the barn, and Dad had put me on Chile and sent me across the slough to bring in the cows. Partway across on the way back, it started to hail. Chile walked carefully through the slough, but as soon as she saw dry land, she bolted for the barn, and I was unceremoniously dumped in the slough. I expect that had something to do with my dislike for horseback riding in later years.

I remember going with Dad to get a load of wood. Heaven knows where we went, but it was in the "bush," and quite a jaunt from home, and it was with team and sleigh to get a load of logs to bring home for firewood. It was a cold but sunny winter day, and I remember riding on the sleigh bunks with my Dad.

We worked hard loading logs, though I doubt I was much help, probably no more than eight or so years of age at the time. But then it was lunch time, so there we sat on the partial load of logs, eating sandwiches and drinking tea, which Mom had made and put in quart jars wrapped in several layers of newspaper.

The tea was still warm as we sat together, two guys having lunch and throwing little pieces of bread crusts to the whiskey jacks. I think the ride home in the dark on top of the logs was a little less enjoyable, but what a wonderful and memorable day.

I remember playing in the ditches in the spring, where water ran like a river sometimes under the snow. I would make little boats out of pieces of wood and follow them along the ditch.

I remember getting wet trying to get through those ditches to get pussy willows. I particularly remember one spring when Ian and Val arrived home soaking wet after going for pussy willows. Both got supreme heck for wading across the ditch. As Ian was getting spanked, he remarked, "The next time Dennis wants pussy willows, he can darn well get them himself."

On the back of this photo, Mom has written, "I think Dennis & I had argued just before this was taken. Lynne & her doll are the only cheerful ones. Gavin was asleep, and we were just ready to leave for church."

I remember going with Dad to Uncle Cliff's when I was about ten or twelve, with a team of horses and a wooden water tank on a sleigh. We had to get water for our cows as our dugout was shallow and frozen to the bottom. It was a nice winter day, but likely about -20 C.

Dad had taken along a 22 rifle to shoot rabbits which were overrunning the country that year. On the way home with a load of water he stopped the team to shoot a rabbit. When the gun went off the team jumped and into the hole on top of the ice-covered tank I went. Dad hauled me out and hurried the team along but I was cold as hell and as stiff as a board by the time we got home. I think Mom might have scolded him that time too, once I got changed, wrapped in a blanket, and parked in front of the open oven door.

I remember falling in the river while helping Uncle Cliff get out ice. He dragged me out by the scruff of the neck and likely saved my life—the water was damned cold!

He let me wait in his old international truck with the heater on while he loaded it alone. For years afterwards, he would jokingly reprimand me about losing a good set of ice tongs in the river. We never did have running water on the farm, and so we put up ice in the winter—packed in lots of sawdust in an ice house—which kept it fairly well frozen for summer use. And no, these ice cubes weren't for drinks. They were about 2 or 3 feet square and were melted for drinking and cooking water, or put in an icebox to keep the milk and butter cool.

This isn't Uncle Cliff, but this shows how the ice was removed from the river. We used a large saw to cut the blocks before removing them. This ice looks rather thin compared to the ice that we put up, which was usually at least two feet thick.

I should mention here that water wells in our area of the Peace River country were almost nonexistent. One family about 12 to 15 miles away had a well with water unsuitable for drinking. Unless you were lucky enough to have a river or creek running through your land, you had to rely on a dugout for watering the animals. Sometimes you could use the water for laundry or bathing, but usually it was not considered clean enough for personal use.

I do remember that we sometimes dragged bluing[3] (in solid form) through the water, which apparently kept down the algae in the water and improved its overall quality. This was a two-person job, with the bluing put in a cloth bag with strings attached so people on each side of the dugout could drag it through the water. We would start at one edge of the dugout, then move the bag over a few

---

[3] From Wikipedia: Bluing has other miscellaneous household uses, including as an ingredient in rock crystal "gardens" (whereby a porous item is placed in a salt solution, the solution then precipitating out as crystals), and to improve the appearance of swimming-pool water. In Australia, it was used as a folk remedy to relieve the itching of mosquito and sand fly bites.

Solid bluing is sometimes used by hoodoo doctors to provide the blue color needed for "mojo hands" without having to use the toxic compound copper sulfate. Some Native American Tribes also used bluing to mark their arrows, showing tribe ownership. (Please refer to Wikipedia for a more detailed definition)

feet and drag it back the other way. We went back and forth until we had the whole dugout covered.

In more recent times, most farms in the area have put in proper filtering systems so the dugout water can be used for regular household use.

I remember a lady from the Family Herald coming to interview Mom, as she had written several articles for various publications. She used an old typewriter we had bought third-hand from Eddy Tjostheim—about 3 years my senior—for me to practice on for my grade 10 typing class. She got paid for most of her articles—I think the tops was $15. Likely, all went to buy school clothes. She never learned to type other than the "hunt and peck" method, but, yes, I can still type with all my fingers…sorta.

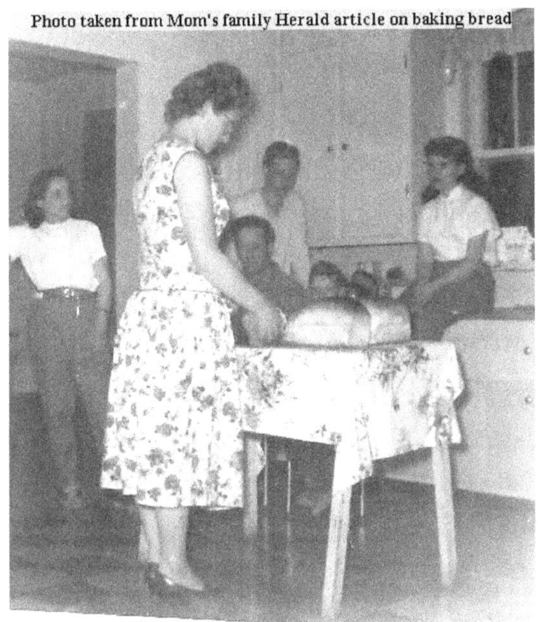

Looks like we should have straightened out the flimsy table leg before the photo was taken.

I remember Grandpa Brown (Mom's Dad) and some of Mom's siblings coming to Nampa with their country show and dance. Grandpa's name was Claude, and his second name was Morgan, and they billed themselves as "C. Morgan Brown and the Brownies."

Grandpa played the violin, the mandolin and the saw, while Wayne and Allen played violin and mandolin, with Uncle Jay on the guitar. My Aunt Hilda usually sang with their group, but wasn't able to come up to the Peace Country with them that year, so Mom filled in as their country singer.

She was a good singer, and I was a proud son. Their show included a minstrel show—that was the comedy routine—in which they blackened their faces with burnt cork—very politically incorrect nowadays, but quite normal in those days. Their show was always followed by a dance—likely the best dance band that ever hit Nampa.

Grandpa's eyesight slowly deteriorated from being gassed in the First World War, and by around the mid-fifties, he was totally blind. He learned to play the piano after he went blind, and was a shrewd card player with his braille cards.

In his later years, until not long before he died, Grandpa used to entertain at several seniors' lodges in Edmonton. (see photos below—circa 1975). Uncle Allen could, in fact, play almost any stringed instrument and was Alberta fiddle champ for several years, starting when he was about 14. Later, he actually spent a couple of years as part of the Wilf Carter (Montana Slim) travelling Show and band.

As I write this, he is about 75 (only 3 years my senior) and can still cut a mean tune on the fiddle—

Orange Blossom Special being my favourite. (Uncle Allen passed away in 2021 at about 84 years of age…the last of my Mom's immediate family)

Every couple of years or so, Grandma and Grandpa Brown would come to Nampa on the train to visit us. Sometimes, the "boys" would come up as well, and a great jam would take place at our house. I loved those days and always hated to go to bed because when the music was done, they would talk far into the night. Often, it was about *their* "good old days" and always involved lots of laughter.

Greetings

At this time, we wish to extend our heartfelt thanks for the privilege it has been to visit you over the years and to have had a small part in bringing entertainment to wonderful friends.

Throughout the coming year our wish for you is the best of everything.

C. MORGAN BROWN
TELEPHONE: 469-3286

Psalms 23:1.—The Lord is my Shepherd; I shall not want.

The Farm Kid and The Flying Bank

I remember working with Uncle Cliff. He and Dad farmed together a lot, and so I spent a lot of time working with him. I liked eating at his place because he always had catsup.

I remember driving his old John Deere tractor, pulling the binder while he sat on the binder to trip the bundle carrier. The tractor had a hand clutch, which, for a kid of about 12, was pretty hard to engage after a stop for something. I had to start the tractor and had to really reef on the clutch, which meant starting with a jerk.

I remember some yelling going on, and I turned around to see Uncle Cliff running to catch up. I guess he had tumbled backward off the seat when I started up. I couldn't hear what he was yelling—likely just as well.

This resembles Cliff's binder, but his was a green John Deere. Easy to see why a man could tumble off the back of it. He should have been hanging on.

I remember getting home from school—likely about Grade 9 or 10—and Mom drove me over to Cliff's, where they were threshing and wanted my help. This usually meant climbing into the bin and shovelling the grain away from the spout so the granary could be filled as full as possible. This was a crappy, dusty job and likely not very healthy.

However, this one time, they decided I could handle a team and a hay rack to gather the bundles in the field and bring them into the threshing machine. It was maybe a quarter mile back to the outfit from the field, and for some reason, I took the trail that was commonly used to get to the field and back—a different route than what they had been using all day.

There appeared to be plenty of room to go between two trees, but before I could change my mind, the horses and wagon were still going, while I and the rack sat on the ground. I believe I was the target of some choice words that day, also.

Similar to our outfit. You can see the straw being blown into a pile, and not so visible is the threshed grain being augured into a granary or wagon box. It appears that this grain is being augured into a truck box. We didn't have a truck. On the left, you can see the long belt, which is driven off the pulley on a tractor.

I remember Dad driving me over to the "other place," a quarter he bought about 5 or 6 miles away and always referred to as "the other place."

Anyway, he had been working over there and wanted me to drive the tractor home. It was an old Allis-Chalmers with no power steering, which sometimes locked and was hard to correct. The old beast had a road gear of about 18 MPH, so I was booting along fairly well when it started to hail. Dad quickly passed me in the car and motioned for me to turn off into the Gronlund place so I could take shelter from the hail. I was likely still going too fast, but as I turned the corner, the steering locked, and I took out the corner fence post along with a couple of hundred feet of fence. I wasn't very popular that day either.

I remember, as a young teenager, getting my first—and I think only—baseball uniform with "Nampa Braves" on the front of the Jersey, and number 8 on the back. But, alas, no name on the back—that would have cost too much, I guess.

We had a great baseball team, but had no league to play in. We did find lots of games, however, at community sports days, Farmers' Days, and the like in the area, and we won the majority of them. We had some good games with teams from places like Reno, Falher, Donnelly, Peace River, Berwyn, and Grimshaw.

For the bigger tournaments, we combined forces with the Reno players. I was never a heavy hitter, but I had a good hitting average. I can only remember one home run—an inside-the-parker—the fielders moved in because they knew I was not a heavy hitter, and I got one over their heads. I played second base and loved the game. Still do.

Dad was a baseball catcher in an old bush league in the Peace River area and was anxious to get me into baseball as well. My first piece of equipment—I think I was seven or eight—was a catcher's mitt.

It was a kid's mitt and pretty much little more than a leather-covered "pad," kind of like a pancake—a far cry from what they use today. I never did become a catcher. I would always close my eyes when the batter swung.

Gavin and me...he has my old "Mitt"

I remember Sunday school and family picnics along the river at Uncle Jim and Aunt Mary's— about a mile and a half north of Nampa, where they lived on the Hart River. Somebody always made ice cream, so we would line up for our scoop or two. Usually, a scrub ball game would take place amongst the cow pies, which we sometimes used as bases—only the dry ones, of course.

I remember, *not* so fondly, Mom's Monday wash days. When we got off the school bus, we would see blue smoke coming from the back of the house, and this meant the old gas-powered washing machine was going.

Dad had rigged up an exhaust system so the washer could be used in what was our "utility room" with the fumes exhausted through a hole in the window frame to the outside.

Washday meant that I would have to haul out the wash water in buckets when she was done. The utility room was meant to be a bathroom someday, but it was still just an unfinished "utility room" when my folks sold out in 1973.

Val says she remembers when we got the new-fangled gas-powered washing machine while we still lived at Cliff's. She remembers it being pulled into the yard behind the little tractor on a stone boat. Her memory is better than mine.

I remember putting up hay with Uncle Cliff and Uncle Jay at our place when I was about twelve. We never did have a baler, so the hay was cut with a mower, then raked into windrows, then picked up with pitchforks and loaded onto a hay rack, which was pulled with horses.

It was an awful job, especially on a hot day. The chaff would go down your neck when you lifted the hay above your head, and every so often, as we unloaded, we would have to jump onto the hay stack and pack it down as best we could.

Anyway, on this particular day, as we were unloading, Uncle Cliff noticed a piece of harness out of place on one of the horses. I don't know what it was called. He asked me to jump off the rack and straighten it out, and having never harnessed a horse, I had no idea what he was talking about.

He lit into me about what kind of a farm kid I could be if I didn't even know that—I still have no idea what he was talking about. I had had about enough of this hay crap as it was, so that was the last straw, no pun intended.

I yelled back, "Then do it your f...ing bloody self," and jumped off the rack and took off. I knew Mom would wonder why I wasn't helping them, so I went out to the road and crawled in the ditch until I got past the house and went up to Uncle Alex and Aunt Millie's place. I did come home for dinner, and not a word was said, but Cliff and Jay kept looking at me, then at each other, and smiling. However, they never said a word to my folks, and that was the end of that.

I remember being within easy biking or walking distance of many of our cousins—all on my

Dad's side of the family—and we travelled back and forth a lot, especially in the summer, and often "slept over" at their place or ours.

The Talbots sometimes rode their horses down to our place, but while I had a pony—Chile—to ride, you now know why I preferred to walk or bike. My cousin Edwin Talbot was only three months younger than I, and we were very close growing up. He was a much better skater than I, but I think I was a better ball player.

The Talbots had a white horse named "Queeny," and they would often ride her the mile or more to our place. I well remember Edwin's younger brother, Neil [4], riding Queeny down on a muddy day with his muddy rubber boots making big "swish" marks on both of Queeny's sides. I don't think Neil was more than about 8 at the time.

"[4]" Sadly, we lost Neil in about 2022 to Pancreatic Cancer. Neil was 75.

My cousin Edwin Talbot and wife Martha visited us in Arizona during the winter of 2007/08.

3

THE EARLY YEARS AT UNCLE CLIFF'S HOUSE

The log house I refer to as "Uncle Cliff's place" is the first home I remember, and it is where we lived when I started school. The house had a sizeable attic, and I remember a number of things being stored up there, some of which I wish we had now.

I expect they were still up there when Uncle Cliff sold the place many years ago, and Lord knows whatever happened to them. I specifically remember an old gramophone with the cylindrical records. I don't think I ever heard it played. It was likely not in working condition but simply stored while Grandma McConnell still lived there.

I also remember a lidded metal box with some old papers and medals in it. I think I remember Dad once saying they were his Uncle Charlie's Orangemen's medals, but I never knew who "Uncle Charlie" was.

The interior of the walls was covered in heavy paper and painted with calcimine, which came in a powdered form and was mixed with water. I thought it only came in white, but Val tells me it could be tinted different light colors—peach, green, buff, etc.

I think we had linoleum floors throughout the house, which included a kitchen, living room and two bedrooms. Joints between the laid linoleum were covered in thin brass colored metal strips that were tacked down. I guess this was to keep the edges of the linoleum from coming up, but I think many a person managed to cut their toes on the metal strips when they became loose or damaged.

The windows were quite low to the ground— how else could I have attacked that moth? As I recall, the logs were chinked on the outside with a mud and straw mixture, and dirt was banked up around the outside of the house for insulation. I remember spending many happy hours playing with the few toys I had on those dirt banks.

Of course, we had no power, telephone, or running water. Our one main light was a gas-fueled mantle lamp, and we had at least one or two coal oil-fueled lamps with glass globes. The globes would get smoked up and had to be cleaned often.

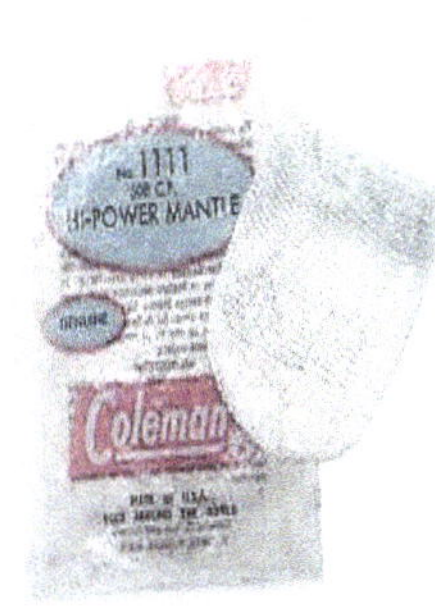

(Left to right:

(1) our main light...two mantles and fueled by "High Test Gas" (I believe this gas is still used for camp stoves). This lamp appears to have no mantles, but they would be attached to the two pipes hanging from the top.

(2) a package of new mantles. They would be tied on with little strings that were attached to the mantle, then lit with a match and "burned." This would shrink them, and they would become very delicate, but they would make a good light when you turned the gas on and lit it.

(3) a coal oil lamp similar to the ones we had. The wick was usually about an inch wide and made of braided cotton. Several inches would hang in the reservoir, and it would be cranked up with the little wheel on the right as it burned down. The wick would draw the fuel up, and the flame would burn at the top of the wick. I have no idea what kept the wick from burning right up. I suppose because they were tightly woven, but they lasted a long time.)

(4) a coal oil lantern. They didn't give a lot of light but this is what we would carry with us to do the chores in the dark...like milking the cows, etc. It operated the same as the coal oil lamp but the flame was enclosed so it wouldn't blow out when you were outside. A little lever lifted the globe a couple of inches so you could light it. The globe on this lantern looks like it is pretty well smoked up.

Water for drinking and cooking was usually melted snow in the winter and ice from the ice house in the summer. Water for bathing, laundry and washing floors and dishes was either from the dugout or snow melt.

We bathed in a fairly big round tub…the girls first and then me…in the same water. No wonder I was kind of a dirty little bugger. We envied some of our neighbors who had an elongated tub…long enough to actually lie down in, but it still had to be filled by hand and emptied the same way.

We had quite a large barn at Cliff's place and several horses and a number of cows…normally one or two for milking…while others were raised for meat or for sale. We also raised pigs from time to time, but Dad was mainly a grain farmer.

World War II ended when I was four, so I can't say that I remember much about it or that I had any concern about the war.

However, I do remember Mom and Dad with their ear to the old Battery radio to catch up with news of the war…and I expect they were particularly concerned about Dad's brothers, Alex and Cliff, who were overseas.

Uncle Alex was, in fact, wounded at least once while overseas, and I recall seeing an embroidered cushion cover that he had made while recuperating in a hospital in England. I vaguely remember them coming home from the war, but my recollections about that are pretty clouded.

Val had to fill me in on the following—in her words:

"After Mom and Dad were engaged, Mom went out to Hilda and Alf's west of Rimbey and stayed one winter.

Dad came with the Model A to get her and bring her back to Nampa. Hilda and Alf moved to Lacombe sometime later. Alf had been the Secretary of the Municipality out west of Rimbey when Mom stayed with them.

When they got married, Grandpa Brown had already joined up and was stationed in Edmonton, so their honeymoon consisted of having Grandma Brown, all the younger kids and their dog packed into the Model A for their trip to Edmonton, where Grandpa had rented them a house.

Mom said they had $200.00 and bought all their household furnishings, lots of grocery staples, etc., before they headed back to Nampa. Apparently, they agonized considerably before breaking down and buying the little battery radio that we had until we got the power!"

I remember Dad telling me that the road to Edmonton was all gravel until they hit pavement about 20 miles from the city. That's when he found out that the wheels were so badly out of line that he could hardly keep the car on the road.

As Dad was opening up more and more land, there were usually roots to be picked, and he would often hire someone to help with this thankless job. More often than not, he would hire indigenous People who came out of the bush from somewhere in the springtime.

They would arrive some spring day with horses pulling a covered wagon, sometimes with a horse or two in tow and usually a dog or two tied under the wagon. I guess the dogs had to keep up or get dragged.

They would find a spot, often along the river somewhere, to pitch their tents and set up camp for the summer. The Ernie Scotti family often pitched their camp just across the road from the gate into our place as Dad hired the same folks several years in a row…to not only pick roots, but also to stook grain bundles in the fall.

They used to get water from our dugout, and I remember one of the girls (Mary, likely about 12), along with her little brother (Raymond) and a pail or two, standing at the gate and yelling for our attention, saying, *"We know where it is, but we are scared of the cows."*

So I, the little 5 or 6-year-old hero, would go down to the gate to accompany them to the dugout and back.

Full-blooded Indigenous men have little or no facial hair. One day Dad took Mr. Scotti to the Nampa Store to buy a few grocery items. Among his selections were several bottles of shaving lotion (which had a fairly high alcohol content). The storekeeper, Mr. Matwek, asked Ernie why he needed so much shaving lotion, to which his reply was, "I shave lots." I think he was restricted to one bottle.

While I cannot personally recall the following incident, Val says she can, and so I am including it here.

One day, an RCMP vehicle, along with a priest, arrived at the Scottis' campsite. As the Scotti kids were not going to school, we wonder now if they were being taken away to a residential school. We never really knew.

Dad did his farming with horses in those early years, but did acquire a used Ford Ferguson tractor sometime before we left Uncle Cliff's place. He also had a Model A car, which got us to where we had to go…mostly to Nampa, about 6 miles away, with no paved roads.

What we called the "main road" (which we later lived on) was almost a mile from Cliff's place. It was sometimes referred to as "the McKinnon Highway," and, although it was not even gravelled, it was kept in much better condition than the one we lived on, which, in the springtime, would become a quagmire and virtually impassable by car.

I can well remember Dad hitching a team to the Model A and driving them with the lines through the front window (which lifted up) and driving to the main road.

To avoid the mud and gumbo, he would drive them on the *other* side of the ditch, and I can still see and hear the willows slapping at the car as we rode over them. When we got to the main road Dad would tie the team to a tree and drive to Nampa...or occasionally to Peace River (some 20+ miles away). The main road took us the 3 miles to the Number 2 Highway, which was gravelled…then two miles south to Nampa, or about 17 miles North to Peace River.

Nampa had two small schools located side by side…one from Grades one to six and one from grades seven to nine. When I started school, there was apparently a shortage of teachers, so our school had a "supervisor." We essentially took correspondence, and she helped with our learning and…of course, our discipline.

That supervisor happened to be Doris Owen, who was my mother's cousin by adoption, and I believe around 18 at the time. Doris was adopted as a young girl by Ab & Edna Owen (Edna being my Grandpa Brown's sister). I think I was a pretty good student thanks to a good back grounding at home.

However, I was a bit unkempt and often had dirty hands…I think not atypical at that time of a young farm kid with no running water at home, although we always had soap and water to wash…it was just not a priority for this kid.

Part of our school regimen was "health inspection," where we were marched across the front of the class…showing our hands to the "supervisor." I was picked as a prime example of uncleanliness, so out came the basin of water and a bar of soap, and Ms. Owen scrubbed and dried one of my hands. Then she had me hold them up to class and asked me, "Which one looks the best?" I held up the dirty hand…I guess I was a little ornery because she had made a spectacle of me.

Anyway…the result was several good slaps with a ruler on the hand…the only time that happened to me, and I held that against her for many years—and I think the feeling was mutual.

In those days, the "strap" was a common part of the school's "teaching" supplies, and some kids over the years got a pretty good beating if caught swearing, etc., although it was always on the hands.

I think that would be a criminal offense in this day and age.

There were about 8 or 10 kids in my grade one class, and I was one of only two or three who actually passed that year. Mind you, the majority of the kids had a first language other than English…mostly Ukrainian or Czechoslovakian, and had to learn English at school.

Many years later, one of the English-speaking kids—who had to repeat Grade One, by the way—had the audacity to suggest that I only passed Grade One because the teacher was related to me.

Grade one is when I had my first lesson in high finance. A classmate, Sharon Hibbard, whose family were friends of ours, told me how I could get a new package of crayons. She said she would just go to Brown's store and ask them to put the crayons on her Dad's bill.

Hot dang…didn't even need any money to buy crayons. So…I went to Brown's store, and they put the cost on Dad's bill—I don't even remember them asking any questions. We are probably talking about seven or eight cents.

Well, when Dad got the bill, that's when I received my first and harsh lesson on finance. I didn't try that again.

The two schools were used for many community activities, but the main activity that I can remember was the Whist Drives. Folks would gather to play the card game "Whist"…I don't know the exact details of their Whist Drives, but I think everyone contributed a dime, and I do remember potatoes cut in half on each table to hold little flags made of toothpicks with a bit of ribbon stuck to them.

The winning pair would move to another table and take a flag or two with them, and at the end of the evening, the one or two people with the most flags would win the "prize(s)".

The women would bring lunch, and coffee was made, and it was a fairly regular social event…mainly in the winter months. Us kids would go along and keep ourselves busy, usually falling asleep on a blanket in a corner somewhere until the folks were ready to leave for home.

I also remember going to these whist drives with a team and sleigh when the weather was very cold. Dad would put lots of straw in the sleigh box and some blankets, and we would all snuggle into them to keep warm. The old Model A was likely put on blocks for the winter, as many of the roads would have been impassable by car anyway.

I also remember going visiting in the winter by the same mode of transportation, and sometimes, as Dad was more exposed to the cold than the rest of us, he would let Mom hold the lines, and he would run behind to warm up. A few folks actually had enclosed cutters with a small wood-fired heater in them, but we didn't have such a luxury.

Our sleigh was like a wagon box on runners that could haul grain or other items.

I also remember going to dances at the Nampa Community Hall as a young kid…In fact, I vaguely remember the hall being built after one had burned down some years earlier. Mom's story at the end of this "book" says the hall burned down in 1938, but here's what Val had to say about that:

"The Nampa Hall I remember burning down was when I was a little kid, so it had to be after 1938. It was on a Farmer's Day when Bertha and BettyAnn, I think, went over to light the gas lamps for the dance, and somehow the fire started. Dad and Uncle Alex had left Aunt Milly, Mom, and us kids at Henry Taylor's place in Nampa while they went home to do chores, and I remember Whilma Taylor bawling when the fire happened. We weren't allowed to go close to have a look, but we knew it was on fire." After that, they built the new hall, which I thought was pretty big until I grew up. Now it looks as though somebody cut it in half. I think it might be a drop in centre now.

Now, are you as confused as me? Mom said the hall burned down in 1938, and as this was where they went to school, they had to finish the year off in the Catholic Church. If Val remembers the hall burning down (and I *vaguely* do), then I'm wondering if the new hall Mom refers to also burned down a few years later. We sure weren't around when Mom was going to school.

A lot of folks would go as a family, and the young ones would play until they were worn out, and it wasn't unusual to see several of us wrapped in blankets sleeping on the stage or under a bench while our parents danced the night away.

More often than not, the dances were in the winter, so we sometimes went to them in the sleigh as well. There was always lunch and coffee at around midnight, and I remember trying to stay awake long enough to get a piece of cake or some cookies.

Sometimes they would have a box social where the ladies would make a lunch and dress up a box to put it in. These were then auctioned off to raise a little money, and the successful buyer then sat with and shared lunch with the lunch maker.

I don't think the women were always happy with their lunch partner, but it was part of the game and all for a good cause. I'm sure some of the single gals gave their favorite guy a hint as to which box they had brought.

I remember my Mom once making a box that looked like a miniature outhouse. I don't recall if Dad was forbidden to see Mom's box creations beforehand, or if it was an unwritten rule that husbands couldn't bid on their wives' lunch boxes.

When I was about 4 or 5—as best as I can recall—we took the train one winter to Edmonton to spend Christmas with Grandpa and Grandma Brown, who lived in Beverley, which is now part of Edmonton.

I remember Grandpa picking us up at the train station in Edmonton with a team and a sleigh. It was a fairly cold day, and most of Edmonton it seemed used coal to heat their homes, and I can still smell the distinct smell of burning coal in the air as we rode in the sleigh to Beverley.

I also remember that I received a balloon from someone, which was the first one I had ever seen.

Of course, the adults had as much fun with it as I did until someone batted it towards the Christmas tree, and it broke. I think I bawled my head off and was mad at whoever did the last bat…I think it was my Mom.

I can also remember the first time I saw bubble gum and when I had my first soft ice cream. I was likely about 7 or so, and we were in Nampa, and I had run over to the old ball diamond to play with some kids.

As I recall, there was a swing or two there, about where the Nampa Post Office is now, and one of the kids on the swing was blowing bubbles. I hadn't seen anything like it before.

I may have been a little older, although I can't really remember, when we were in Peace River one day. There was an empty lot on Main Street, kitty corner from the theatre, and a little building was set up, and they were selling soft ice cream.

Dad sprang for a cone for all of us—likely no more than a dime each. What a miraculous invention. I was in Peace River in July 2013, and that lot is still empty (or empty again??), alas, no ice cream vendor.

4
A NEW HOME...

When Mom and Dad bought the land in 1945, it was only a quarter of a mile from the Trowsdale school, so they thought that would be handy for us when we started school.

Unfortunately, it was abandoned as a school before I entered Grade one, so I had to start school at Nampa. It was a one-room schoolhouse, and I believe it served Grades 1 to 6.

Copies of old school registers in the Nampa History book showed up to 22 students attending. After its school days were over, it was sometimes used for community events and, in particular, country dances.

As was not unusual then, there was usually a lot of drinking outside the hall, and this sometimes led to fist fights. *(As Peggy points out, in those days you drank outside and smoked inside, whereas that is now reversed.)*

Ian and I would often go up to the school the day after to gather beer bottles, which we could sell for a few cents.

One time Ian found a Five Dollar Bill (big money in those days)…no doubt lost from somebody's pocket during a fight.

Anyway, he took it home and gave it to his Dad, and I thought how silly that was. Just think of all the pop and chocolate bars we could have bought.

A few years after we moved into our new home, the Trowsdale school was demolished (or moved—can't remember which). However, the old school barn was still there for many years, and Ian and I once built a secret *man cave* in it. I think the construction was the fun part because I don't remember spending much time there once it was done.

Trowsdale School, circa 1940

About a year after Mom and Dad bought their
first quarter of land in 1945, we moved to that
quarter and spent a year or more living in the old
Gronlund house…a small log home with a later but
still small lumber-built addition. The lumber-built

part was later hauled close to our new home and used, at different times, as a shop and a chicken coop. Mostly, it just collected junk.

It was while we were living in the old Gronlund house that Dad bought his first new car, a 1947 Ford Super Deluxe V8. During the war years, the car manufacturers devoted their time and money towards the war effort, and it was all but impossible to buy a new car. In fact, when Dad ordered his car (in blue), there was a waiting period of several months. It then came as quite a surprise to us when he went to Peace River one day and came home with a new black car.

Apparently, somebody else had ordered a car before Dad did, but then couldn't pay for it when it arrived, so when he went to the Ford dealer in Peace River to check on a delivery date, they said he could drive it home "today" if he didn't mind black.

This was our family car until about the year I left home in 1959, and it was the car that both Mom and I learned to drive on.

It was a three-speed standard transmission with the shifter on the steering column. If my memory serves me right, I don't think it even had a radio—a pretty luxurious item in those days.

The remains of the car were still sitting in the bush on the farm when Mom and Dad sold out in 1973.

Val & Lynne (Lic. Plate on car says 1949) and Gavin in about 1954 (Boy he either had big feet or those were my shoes).

In all of our homes, we used firewood for cooking and heating until we got electricity in the new home in the late fifties. Even then, we still used wood and, later on, coal for heating.

From an early age, it was always my job to keep the wood supply up. At the old Gronlund house, we had a bit of a wooden box just outside the door where it was my job to keep the wood supply for the night.

One night, I had just gone to bed when Dad reminded me that I hadn't filled the wood box and got me unceremoniously out of bed to get it done. I was deathly afraid of the dark—I was only 6 after all—but Dad said if I just got two blocks of wood, he would get the rest.

Out I went, as the door closed behind me and coyotes and wolves licked their chops. Well...what a streak of luck…there were already two blocks in the wood box. So I stood just outside the door for a few minutes, then came in and went back to bed.

Apparently Dad knew those two blocks were already there, so I was out of bed again and out into the dark among the wild and dangerous animals to get some wood. "Prior to purchasing an electric range we, as with most folks in the area, depended on a wood burning cook stove. Some of our neighbors had Propane gas stoves but that was a luxury we never had.

For reasons I never understood my Dad never had me cut kindling (finely chopped slivers of wood) to start the fire for the day. As most campers will know, it is considerably easier to start a fire with kindling than with blocks or larger pieces of wood. My Dad, instead, would almost always start the cook stove fire by throwing some gas on the split wood and throw in a lit match. My Dad slept in the nude and lit the fire the same way. The fire would start with a "whoosh" and was not a good practice, but a quick way to start the fire. I don't recall his ever getting burned but that might explain why he never had hair on his chest.

The summer of 1948, while we lived in the old Gronlund house, Dad was busy building the new house about a quarter of a mile east on the same quarter. Concrete forms for the basement were built on the spot and held together about 6 inches apart with wire run through them at regular intervals, with the wire wound on small pieces of board on each side to hold the forms together while they poured concrete.

I remember Dad hiring the Sherris brothers (Doug and Mel), ,5, who lived just east of the Trowsdale school, to cut all the wires that protruded from the concrete after it had set and the forms were removed. The concrete was all mixed in the yard in a small cement mixer and dumped in the forms by wheelbarrow. No Cement trucks in the vicinity in those days. It was a pretty slow and difficult process.

5. (I think they would have been about 12 and 14 at the time. They both went on to become school teachers, and Doug passed away where he lived near Didsbury, Alberta, in 2020. We did have a couple of visits from Doug once we moved to Carstairs)

Dad hired Mr. Ned Bachmeier from Peace River as lead carpenter and Ewald Sorbey, a neighbor, to do the brickwork for the chimney.

Insulation was all wood shavings...and it wasn't pink. This new home included a cistern in the basement with a hand pump mounted on our sink. The cistern was made of concrete with walls about 6 inches thick and about 10 x 10 ft., and about 5 or 6 ft. High. It would catch the rainwater from our roof, and the hand pump would deliver it to the sink for washing and cooking. I think we even used it for drinking water until one year Dad decided to let the cistern run dry and clean it out.

That's when we found a couple of drowned mice at the bottom, so that was the end of the drinking water.

Also, as we lived on a dirt road (later gravelled), a lot of dust gathered on the roof, so we wound up with about 4 inches of mud in the bottom of the cistern.

That summer, Aunt Hilda visited us from Lacombe, along with my cousins Marv, Neva, and Alfred. Of course, we had this new car ...and it was black...and I had brought some chalk home from school. Marv and I decided we could use the car as a blackboard, and then wipe the chalk off, and no harm would be done.

Who knew that chalk scratches? I think our relatives had gone home by the time Dad discovered the scratches on the car trunk, and of course, I blamed it on Marvin. But Dad, being the detective he was, wouldn't buy my story, and I think I got a bit of a whuppin over that. I expect that he didn't believe my story because the scratches clearly said "Dennis."

While Marvin was visiting, we spent a lot of time at the new house…likely getting in the way, but we decided to use the lumber scraps to build a cabin in the bush not far from the new house. We may have been guilty of sneaking the odd good piece of lumber, but I can't remember for sure.

What I do remember is getting supreme heck (and perhaps a licking"…can't remember) for using up about 5 pounds of nails to build it, and another five pounds of shingle nails to shingle it.

It was a great little cabin…just large enough for the two of us and had a nice metallic shine to it…which later turned to rust. Go figure.

But we weren't the only ones getting into trouble. We had a rain barrel at the old Gronlund place for washing, etc. One day, Lynne and Alfred, who would have been about 3 at the time, got busy picking chickweed, which was in abundance in the yard and topped off the rain barrel with it. No big harm done, but they weren't too popular that day.

We moved into the new house in the summer of 1948. There were four bedrooms upstairs, of which two were never finished. One very large bedroom was for the girls, the other for me.

I did have to share the room for a few years with my little brother Gavin, but I left home when he was eight, so then it was his room. Our two bedrooms were eventually finished, but neither ever had a door.

Of course, I was determined to keep the girls out of my room, so, unknown to my folks, I found an old door off a shack someplace which I dragged upstairs and, using old shoe leather for hinges, nailed it on. I don't think it stayed there for long, though.

Of the two unfinished bedrooms, neither was used for much other than a little storage, although two Indigenous fellows working for Dad did stay in one of the rooms for a while. As I recall, we had a couple of cots they slept on.

Mom used to refer to one of the unfinished upstairs rooms as the "guest room" and the other as the "bathroom." Wishful thinking, I guess.

My Mom had RH-negative blood, and as is apparently normal in such cases, the firstborn is healthy, and each subsequent child has a progressively worse case of jaundice. That meant I was a healthy baby, but apparently, Val was somewhat jaundiced, Lynne much more so, but they survived. The next two babies were either stillborn or died shortly after birth.

By the time Gavin was born in March 1951, medicine had advanced enough to know how to deal with this problem. The day he was born, a nurse took Gavin by plane to Edmonton for an immediate blood transfusion. I think his stay there was about 10 days, and Dad took the train to Edmonton to bring him home by air. This was Dad's first airplane ride—I think it would have been an old DC3.

Uncle Fred Hebert drove us to the airport, which was a few miles across the river from Peace River town, and I can still see that little silver glint in the sky that grew bigger and bigger until we could actually make out that it was a plane. Now we could see our little brother for the first time.

A memorable part of the trip that day is that, for some reason, the bridge was closed (for repairs, I guess), and so an ice crossing had been used all winter. However, by the middle of March, the weather had warmed up considerably, and there were several inches of water on the ice crossing…kind of scary, but it was obviously safe.

I remember that we climbed up the bank on our side of the river, right about where the Peace River Museum still stands. In fact, we were there a few years ago (at our T.A. Norris Reunion), and we could still see that approach road, albeit pretty much grown over.

Of course, I remember the Christmases that always involved getting up about five or six in the morning to check out our presents. It was always the rule that we could have our stockings, which always had a mandarin orange in the toe, some hard candy and nuts, and one small toy...perhaps only a balloon or two, with no present opening until Mom and Dad were up. I expect we pestered them until they got up fairly early themselves.

One year, before we had electricity, Dad rigged up a trouble light off a car battery and had it strategically placed under the tree. When he heard us coming down the stairs, he hooked it up and lit up the tree…our first Christmas light.

My favorite toy growing up, bar none, was a Meccano set for which I sometimes got additional pieces in subsequent Christmases. It seemed there was no end to my engineering skills. I even remember building an oil rig for the back of one of my Tonka trucks. I don't know if they still sell these…kids today are probably too busy with video games to bother with something like that. Meccano was a structural toy with lots of metal pieces that were put together with tiny nuts and bolts. The appropriate tools were part of the set.

When I was in grade two, the Catholic Church brought in a new priest from Quebec. He was, of course, a French Canadian and soon after, large French families began moving into the Nampa area from Quebec, and it wasn't long before they almost outnumbered the rest of us. When I say big families, I mean big…some had 18 or 20 kids.

Most knew little or no English when they arrived, but they learned fairly quickly, and I even learned some French words from them…But I don't think they were the kind of words my mother would be proud of.

I guess there was still a shortage of teachers, so at one point, a nun from Quebec was hired to teach in Nampa. This was the cause of a real uproar, and due to the hue and cry from the non-Catholics, she wasn't there for long. I dare say my Dad was one of those expressing their objection. In fact, so many French folks moved to the area that they eventually established their own communities…specifically the villages of Marie Reine just north west of Nampa, and St. Isadore…now a thriving community just south of Peace River town.

As we grew up, many of those French kids whom we resented at first became good friends, although I don't keep in touch with any of them.

Well…let me clarify that. When I was in Grade nine, I had a crush on this pretty little blonde by the name of Annette Laliberte. Her family lived no more than about a quarter mile from the school. I had a ball game one evening, and had to kill time after school and before game time, and Dad would pick me up after the game.

Annette invited me to spend that time at her place until the game started. I don't know if I was welcomed by her parents or not, but I wound up spending the whole time helping her wash windows.

That was about as close as I came to having a date with her.

I think she was a grade below me, but in any case, she wound up going to a separate school in Peace River, and we went our separate ways, and that was that.

However, I went to a High School reunion in Peace River in 2010, and who should I run into but Annette? As she was by herself, we invited her to sit with us, and we did a lot of reminiscing. Unfortunately, she has had a pretty tough life, losing both of her brothers at a fairly early age— one by drowning and one with diabetes. She was unable to have children, and her first marriage ended in divorce, and her second husband died quite young (or was it the other way around?), and Annette herself was battling cancer for the second time.

We have not been in touch since, so I have no idea if she beat it or not. She did not attend our 2013 Reunion.

Val has already told you how we got to school in Peace River when I was in Grade 3 and her in Grade 1. By the next school year, the new school in

Nampa was built, and we were among the first students to attend.

It was very modern... sort of. There was no plumbing in Nampa in those days, so the school had large outdoor toilets—one for girls and one for boys. Each had several "holes" but no heat, so it was a cold place to sit in the winter. And no gymnasium…Although I believe they got one many years later.

Val could likely tell you who all the teachers were, but I don't remember many of them. I do recall that there were several classrooms, so most grades had their own home room, although the school still went only to Grade 9…after which we had to go to Peace River for High School.

I think I was in about Grade 6 here and Val in Grade 4—just guessing.

We were now living in the "new" house, and fortunately, the living room had a big window facing east, so in the inclement weather, one or some of us would stand at the window watching for the school bus, which by this time was a *real* school bus. Someone would yell, "Here it comes," and there would be a mad scramble to get out the door and to the gate for pickup.

In the summer, pretty well every recess and lunch hour meant playing scrub ball. To me, it was always the best part of school.

In Grade 6, my teacher was Mr. McLean, and he started us doing a little woodwork with a coping saw (or fret saw). All by hand, of course...certainly no power tools, and our school certainly did not have a shop. I still have a wooden silhouette of a moose that I made in that class, which hung in Mom and Dad's home for many years, and in Dad's room at Heritage Towers after that.

It became mine when Dad passed away. (see photo)

I also did some minor woodwork at home, including cutting out letters from quarter-inch plywood to make name signs for the gate. We had one at the "new" house for as long as I can remember.

I also made one for Uncle Cliff and one for Uncle Ed Brown (Grandpa Brown's brother). I expect they all eventually became firewood. I always thought I would like getting into doing more woodworking of some kind, but never did until about 2010, when we had to come home from Arizona for Peggy's new hip.

I didn't know how I would keep myself busy for three months, being used to golfing, card playing, and Happy hours in Arizona, so…I got some tools and patterns, and it has kept me busy ever since.

The Farm Kid and The Flying Bank

We always looked forward to the local "Farmers' Day" at the Nampa school grounds—I think around the first weekend in June. There were ball games, horseshoe tournaments, and lots of games for the kids. And ice cream and watermelon and hot dogs. Oh yes…the highlight…someone would donate a young pig that would be covered in lard, and a "greased pig race" would ensue with the pig going to whoever could catch it.

More than once, I thought I had it, only to wind up with my face in the dirt and covered with grease. As a teenager, I played in some of those ball games. But when we were younger, Mom and Dad would pay us 5¢ a row to weed the garden, and that would be our spending money for Farmers' Day.

Mind you, in those days, I think ice cream was about 5¢ a cone. As youngsters, we would usually arrive home covered with dirt (and sometimes grease) and sticky from the treats we had, but it was always a fun day.

One of the highlights of our school year was the annual track meet. It meant a day or two off school, and we either took a school bus to Reno (about 10 miles away) or the Reno kids were bussed to Nampa.

I was never very big or very strong, but could run pretty well. We competed in things like the 100-yard dash, high jump, long jump, hop, skip and jump, javelin throw, and shot putt. Sometimes a ball game between the two schools was arranged. That is what I looked forward to in particular, but I did bring home a number of ribbons from the track and field events.

Church was part of life, and every Sunday, barring terrible weather conditions, we attended Sunday school and church at the United Church in Nampa. Of course, if it was a busy time of year for Dad…seeding or harvest…he would stay home and work.

I can't remember much about going to church in the very early years, but once Mom learned to drive the new car, she would take us kids if Dad didn't go.

We were brought up right, and swearing was not at all acceptable.

However, as Val reminded me recently, I once used a curse word in Mom's presence. She scolded me and added, *"You never hear your father talking like that."* My response was *"You've never helped him load pigs."*

The Farm Kid and The Flying Bank

Many winters we endured 50 below Fahrenheit (-46 C) or colder weather and lots of snow, and the wind would pile up in drifts several feet deep in places.

We would get the occasional warming spell, which would melt the snow on top a bit, and then when it froze again, it was plenty hard enough to hold a man. We would play on top of the drifts, or burrow under them, or cut hard blocks of snow to build igloo-like structures.

I don't think the winters are nearly as severe nowadays. Roads would sometimes be blocked for quite a while, but fortunately, we lived on a school bus route, so our road was usually cleared fairly quickly.

Of course, with no power, we could not plug in the car, so Dad used to get a metal pot of gas or coal oil, light it on fire, and place it under the oil pan on the car to warm up the oil so the motor would crank over. While the car had antifreeze, the tractor, for some reason, did not.

So, in addition to putting a fire under the tractor, he would fill the radiator with hot water once he thought it was ready to start, and that usually worked.

Of course if it didn't start right away he had to drain the radiator promptly or the engine block would freeze and break.

One winter, Uncle Alex and family lived in the Haack place just east of us—where the Sherris' had lived previously—and one day, when I was likely about nine or ten, I went up to spend the night with Ian.

They had the kitchen table in front of a window that faced the road, with a wooden bench behind the table under the window. As traffic was infrequent on our road in those days, the sound of a vehicle coming in or going by was always a matter of interest.

Well, we heard a vehicle coming, so Ian and I jumped up on the bench so we could see out the window. The bench tipped, and I fell backwards onto Aunt Millie's old sewing machine that was on the table and was impaled in the bum by the spool holder. It hurt like heck and bled a bit, and of course, Aunt Millie was insistent on delivering first aid.

Much to my reluctance and embarrassment, I finally agreed, but first lay on the bed on my belly and had Ian cover me completely except for a few square inches where the wound was.

So she went to work with her peroxide and band aids, and I survived. I likely still have a scar there, but my neck won't bend far enough to check.

From the time I was about eight, it was my job to chop wood and keep the home supplied with wood for cooking and heating. In fact, when I went to camp when I was eleven, I had to chop enough firewood to last until I got home.

Our basement was never finished ...just a concrete floor and walls, and in the severely cold weather Dad allowed me to haul in the wood blocks and split them in the basement. We still had no electricity, and it was always dark by the time we got home from school, so I would put a coal oil lamp on the stairs for light.

One evening, as I was chopping wood, there was a terrible crash at the other end of the basement…where it was very dark. This scared the devil out of me, so I ran up the stairs at top speed, and as I rushed past the lamp it blew out…thereby heightening the terror.

When I arrived upstairs breathless and shaking, Dad took control of the matter. He said, "Let's go have a look." So he headed downstairs with me following timidly behind him. He relit the coal oil lamp and started exploring the basement, and I can still hear him saying, *"Well… haven't seen any bears down here…perhaps there's a whale in the cistern."*

It turns out that earlier in the week, I had been playing in the basement and stacked up a bunch of Mom's canning jars, and the vibration of my wood chopping caused them to fall and break. Boy…I never lived that one down.

That was one of the years that Dad worked in the far northern region of the province as an Oilfield mechanic. I had remembered him telling us that he often saw packs of wolves.

As was customary, all of us kids would write him letters. One of my letters ended with my drawing of a man being chased by a wolf. When I eventually got a letter back from Dad, his letter ended with his drawing of me being chased by a fruit jar. That was my Dad!

One day, our whole family had gone somewhere in the car and returned home just about dusk. As we drove into the yard, a black bear bounded out of it into the nearby bush. When the

The Farm Kid and The Flying Bank

land was cleared, Dad had left a shelter belt of trees all around the farm yard. I'm not sure why, but Dad decided that he had to shoot the bear, so he ran into the house—leaving the rest of us in the car he grabbed his old single-shot .22 and headed out after the bear.

We heard a shot or two and lots of crashing about in the bush, not knowing which was Dad and which was the bear. We had all got out of the car, thinking we would make a dash for the house, and Mom finally yelled, *"Where are you, Gordon, and where is the bear?"* He yelled back, *"Somewhere between me and you."*

You never saw a grown woman and four kids scramble back into a car so fast. As I recall, he looked the next morning and found a few spots of blood, but the bear got away.

Speaking of bears…at around the same time (perhaps a year or two later), our barn had not yet been built, so Dad kept a sow in the old run-down barn near the Gronlund house.

She had just had a sizeable litter of piglets, and one morning Dad went down to feed and water them. Sometime overnight, a bear had entered the barn—there wasn't really much to keep him out.

He ate or carried off two or three of the little pigs and had eaten about 20 pounds out of the sow's shoulders. She was still alive but in obvious pain and distress, so he had no option but to put her down.

I cannot remember how many, if any, of the little pigs survived, but I do know that we used one for bait.

Next to the old barn Dad built a bit of a slab enclosure, penned in the little pig at the far end, and planted a bear trap at the entrance.

We would take turns standing watch at night with rifles ready, waiting for the bear to return, but he never did—he could probably smell us and kept his distance.

I remember doing one shift with Uncle Jay, and I was a bit afraid but excited at the same time. But, alas, no bear showed up.

After a couple of nights of luckless hunting, Dad pulled the old sow into some bush just outside the west edge of our home quarter, figuring the bear would return to chow down.

When he checked the next day, the bear had, indeed, been there, so we knew he was hanging around. Within a day or so Dad had arranged a "posse" to track the bear down…arranged with neighbors and Jay and Wayne and Cliff to wait until evening, then approach the area where the sow was from different angles, hoping to scare the bear out into the opening.

This did the trick. Dad and Wayne were on our little Ford tractor driving through some adjacent land, when the bear suddenly ran across the trail in front of them.

As Wayne related later… *"Gordon stood up from the tractor seat and shot the bear while the tractor was still moving."*

They dragged the bear home, and it sat in our yard near the highway for a couple of days...I suppose to show it off to the neighbors and the like.

I recall it making growling sounds once in a while, which scared me at first, until I learned it was just gases building up inside the bear and escaping from some orifice.

It wasn't long before it started to stink, so Mom had Dad haul it away…I think it wound up next to the old sow.

5
THE ADOLESCENT YEARS

As alluded to above, I loved playing baseball, and Dad encouraged me in this respect. In fact, he helped coach our team at times and, when he couldn`t help out due to farm demands, he would let me drive the little Ford Tractor to Nampa to play ball. I think he would have put a stop to that, however, if he knew the whole story.

Often, after the ball game, two or three of my friends would pile on the tractor, some straddling the hood, and I would bomb around town. It's a wonder nobody fell off and got hurt or killed.

There was no TV in those days, and Major League baseball was not broadcast on the radio, at least not that we could pick up, except for the World Series. The only thing that kept Dad from listening to the World Series was if there was harvest to do…otherwise, his ear was glued to the radio at World Series time.

From the time I was about eleven or twelve, I was expected to help out in the fields. More often than not, this meant driving the old Allis Chalmers and pulling a one-way to summer fallow the fields.

As I have mentioned, the steering was difficult and more than once, while turning at the end of the field, it would lock up, and then the one-way would jack-knife on me. I would have to shut off the tractor, walk home and get Dad to help me out of the predicament.

It usually meant bringing out a chain, unhooking, then pulling the one-way to straighten it out, then hooking it up again and away I would go…until the next time. Dad was never very impressed. I think one-ways have gone the way of the dodo birds…Farm machinery used today is so much larger and more efficient.

this is a tired old "One-Way". Ours was green and about 8 ft. wide

But by and large, I enjoyed driving the little Ford tractor. It was easy to steer and had a good road gear as well. But one time, Dad sent me to the "other place" with the little Ford and a two bottom plow to plow down some alfalfa land. Man was that slow going…can you imagine plowing about 100 acres with a plow that couldn't have been more than about 3 feet across?

Every once in a while, I would hitch the little Ford to our rubber-tired wagon to haul garbage of all kinds down to near the old Gronlund house, where we had a "dumping ground." Mom was constantly warning me to be careful and drive more slowly lest I have an accident.

One day at the "dumping area," I tried backing up the trailer and got hung up in some trees and had to walk home to get help from Dad. When Mom saw me come back on foot, she asked me where the tractor was, and my response was, "I guess you were right, I rolled the darned thing in the ditch." I thought this was funny until she started crying, so then I felt bad and had to fess up.

Then she was mad. And my Mom had above normal hearing. One day, we argued about something…no idea what, but it was something she wanted me to do, and I wasn't happy about it. I walked out of the house, slammed the door, and said, "Why don't you do it your bloody self?" The door was immediately yanked open, and did I ever get it…How did she hear me?? One of those wonders of nature, I guess.

My Dad was never a big farmer, owning only two quarters of land, and while the land in the Peace Country could grow great crops, it was always very dependent on the weather.

Some years it wouldn't quit raining, so they couldn't get on the fields to harvest, sometimes it was too dry, and the crops didn't produce much, and sometimes a killer frost would hit before the grain matured. Farming with older and smaller equipment, it was a bit of a risky business, and many years on the farm were pretty lean.

One year Dad and Uncle Fred Hebert rented a half section of land, and as they didn't use fertilizer in those days, had the expense of summer fallowing it all one summer. The next year, they had a bumper crop of barley, but then the rains started, and they just could not get on the land.

The following spring, they managed to get a hopper full of "chicken feed." Uncle Fred Hebert worked as a mechanic in the oil patch during the winter, and I remember him suggesting to Dad that he should give that a try.

Well, he did…and although he was not a certified mechanic, he had a good head for mechanics and wound up spending approximately 20 winters (from about 1951 to 1971) working "in the bush" for various oil companies. I think originally for "Pik Development" but most often for Chevron, as I recall.

This ensured that we always had food on the table, a good home, and a decent car to drive. He would sometimes be away for a month or more at a time, and we always looked forward to his days off…although with no real way of communicating, it was sometimes a surprise when he arrived.

I remember the girls climbing all over him when he got home, while I stood back…not because I was not happy to have him home, but because I was afraid I would get too emotional. Nobody likes a crybaby.

Sometime in the early fifties, we got a telephone. Dad, along with several neighbors strung lines along fences and the like to connect a number of homes in the area. A neighbor, Logan Sherris, had some experience in this type of work, so he led the operation. We were on a party line, and when we wanted to contact someone on the line, we used a crank on the phone to ring a certain number of short and long rings—everyone on the line had their own specific series of rings…I cannot remember what our ring was, but something like two longs and a short.

Of course, anyone could listen in on others' calls, so a lot of rubbernecking went on. If we needed to make a long-distance call, we would ring the Nampa Store, where they would manually connect us to the main grid.

Before we finally got electricity, we still used a mantle gas lamp, which most often hung in the doorway between the kitchen and living room. It was above our heads as kids, but the adults had to duck around it. More than once, somebody would run into it and knock it down. No harm done other than the mantles had to be replaced, but we were lucky the house didn't catch on fire.

We also had a couple of coal oil lamps—the kind with a wick and a glass globe, which we often carried from room to room as needed. In fact, we did lots of homework by the light of one of those.

One day, when I got home from school, I was taken to task for almost burning the house down. I had lit one of the lamps in my bedroom that morning and laid the match (flame out but still hot,

I guess) on a plastic-like cover on the top of my dresser. I guess it smouldered for awhile and by the time Mom or Dad smelled smoke, the whole top of my dresser had burned.

Sometime in the mid to late fifties, we finally got "power." I don't know where Dad got his wiring knowledge from, but he got a permit and wired the house himself. He managed to fish wire through the walls…even those insulated with shavings, so the job was completed without the necessity of any "surface wiring."

He had some 12 volt light bulbs and tested every plug, switch, and light fixture by hooking up a car battery at the fuse box, and so passed the subsequent electrical inspection without a hitch. It seemed like a long wait for the power to be hooked up, but we were ready when it arrived. Val reminded me that the first electrical appliance bought was a clock radio. And one of the first things Dad bought for himself was an electric drill. I have no idea why an electric stove was not high on the priority list, but that wasn't purchased until I left home…no one to split the wood then, I guess. However, a refrigerator was one of the early purchases.

The Farm Kid and The Flying Bank

Sometime during my junior high years, we bought a new space heater that stood in the living room and was fired mainly with coal. I no longer needed to haul in wood blocks for the heater, but it still involved manual labour…or should that be boy labour?

Dad would have a load of coal delivered through a basement window, where it was piled up and still had to be hauled to the upstairs heater in a coal bucket. The advantage over wood was that it would burn longer, and it alleviated the need to get up during the night to stoke the heater.

Shortly after Dad bought his electric drill, Mom wanted to wallpaper their bedroom, which was adjacent to the kitchen.

In those days, the paper did not come prepasted; rather, paste had to be mixed in a pail and "painted" onto the back of the wallpaper.

The glue was pretty hard to mix, so Dad got the great idea of mixing it with his drill. He got a heavy piece of wire and fashioned a mixer for the drill. He stuck it in the pail and pulled the trigger, and instantly the glue flew from the pail and covered most everything in the kitchen. I think Mom went for a long walk and said she would be back when

Dad got the mess cleaned up. The mixer was not unlike some you can buy today, but obviously Dad's invention wasn't very symmetrical.

The doors to our house never had proper locks on them, and, with Dad being away all winter, Mom and I were always a bit nervous, so we would put chairs in front of the doors at night, and I slept in the living room on a cot near the front door. Don't know what I would do if intruders showed up, but as I was about 14 or so at the time, I was the man of the house.

Late one night, Dad came home unexpectedly and found the doors barred and couldn't arouse any of us. I guess he banged on their bedroom window to no avail. He finally forced his way in through the front door, and I never woke up until he was in the room. Some protector I was.

One winter, two of our neighbors went missing. George Craig, who lived about a mile and a half from us, along with Shorty Sherris, had a cabin in the bush quite a ways east of us that they used for hunting and trapping. Their mode of transportation at that time was Mr. Craig's little Ford tractor, and when they didn't show up at home when they were supposed to, folks began to worry.

The Farm Kid and The Flying Bank

When some local men went to check on them, they found the cabin burned down with one body inside that they concluded was George Craig, and speculation was that they had had a fight and Shorty had killed George and took off on the tractor.

At a later search of the area, in which my Dad was involved, Shorty's body was subsequently found a short distance into the bush. Both had been shot to death, and their tractor was missing.

Not too long afterwards, the murderer, a Mr. Alfred, who was also trapped in the area, was found in Grimshaw (about 35 miles away) with the tractor keys in his pocket. As I recall, they found him eating in a restaurant. Anyway, he was charged with the murders, and I believe he was one of the last persons in Alberta to be executed by hanging.

Considering the above note, where my Dad had to literally break into our house, it is somewhat ironic that we later calculated that Mr. Alfred almost certainly drove right past our house with the tractor on his escape route on one of those nights.

Note: this anecdote was put together as my sister Valerie and I remember it, and is not the "Official" story.

One of my friends in Junior High at Nampa was Jack Hibbard. He was a grade below me, but we got along well. I think we were about thirteen and fourteen when I convinced Mom to let me go camping overnight with Jack. We found a spot near the river, pitched a small tent and had a great time hiking in the bush, making slingshots and doing whatever young kids did in those days to pass the time.

We had brought along a couple of inner tubes and were going to do some tubing on the river, which, for the most part, was quite shallow. Things started off well, but I had drifted only a few feet when I decided to jump off and get a better bum hold on the tube.

Little did I know that where I jumped off the water was over my head, and I panicked. The Hibbard kids, and especially Jack, were pretty good swimmers, and when he realized the trouble I was in, he tried to help me. Of course, I was struggling to keep my head above water, so I was virtually climbing on him and, without realizing it, was holding him under water.

To his credit, however, he managed to save me, and I remember him laying on the bank puking up water. I was fine because I held my head above the water for the most part, but I did feel sorry for Jack. The next morning, that event was forgotten about, and we even got a fire going and cooked some bacon and eggs that we had taken along…or was it eggs and hot dogs?? before we headed for home.

One day, a few years later, when I was in High School, I heard that Jack had been involved in a terrible accident. He and another one of our friends, Germaine Durand, were hunting squirrels not far from Nampa and, as I heard it, Jack was banging on a tree with his rifle butt to scare out a squirrel when his gun went off.

Unfortunately, he hit Germaine in the stomach, and it took some time for Jack to run for help and for someone to get Germaine to the hospital, by which time he had bled to death. It was an accident, but I'm sure Jack never got over that.

I graduated from Grade nine in 1956 as tops in my class. Mind you, there were only nine of us, and most were kids who knew no English when they started school, including the French kids who moved in a few years earlier.

Most of them were quite intelligent…they just had a rougher start, and many of them were very successful later in life.

So…now I was done with the Nampa School and on to Grade 10 in Peace River. That's when I found out I wasn't so smart after all.

6

THE HIGH SCHOOL YEARS

Grade 10...September of 1956. A new school and lots of new classmates.

Now I had to walk the almost two miles to the number 2 highway as the bus to Peace River originated at Reno and picked up kids along the highway only.

In the summer I rode my bike and ditched it at Percy Talbots place at the intersection, or more often just kind of hid it in the culvert. Come winter, however, it was shank`s pony - in the dark each way.

I quite honestly can't remember missing a day because of bad weather, although in the bitterly cold weather we listened to the radio and would find out if the school bus was running or not. I was still a bit afraid of the dark and there were reports of coyotes with rabies in the area so dad actually let me carry the 22 rifle with me and it, too, was stashed in the culvert until I got off the bus for the walk home.

When I was in Grade Eleven my good friend, Peter Cruickshank who was a grade behind me, would walk with me. He lived two miles further down the road so had a four mile walk every morning and every night. He would make it to our place in time to come in and warm up before we headed out for the last stretch.

I can`t remember if it was the fall of 1957 or the spring of 1958 when they paved the highway. I do remember getting off the bus with Peter and we got on our bikes and had to have a few spins on the new pavement.... that is until an RCMP officer came along and gave us what for.

Peter was a very bright student and I think he had just started grade eleven when he was diagnosed with Tuberculosis. This meant he was sent to Edmonton to spend part of his life quarantined in a sanatorium, as was the custom in those days.

Peter missed a lot of schooling because of this but later moved to Edmonton and became a successful businessman. He was a great friend who died much too young at 65 due to cancer.

The school known as "T. A. Norris High" had just been built and ours was the first class of grade ten kids in that school. The Grade eleven and twelve's who had gone to the old Peace River High School were transferred to T. A. Norris as well. It was pretty overwhelming...a strange school, strange kids, strange teachers, and two rooms just for the grade 10's. And not only that we had to shift class rooms almost every period for different courses and different teachers.

However, it didn't take too long to make some good friends...most of whom were country kids like me...some of them from the other side of the river...Ian Garstin being the one I probably chummed with the most. His folks farmed west of Peace River at Weberville. Ian joined the Bank of Nova Scotia about the same time as I started working for the Canadian Bank of Commerce so we have done lots of reminiscing at various T. A. Norris reunions.

Note: T. A. Norris was a high school for 10 or 12 years only...from the mid fifties to the mid 60's. Therefore, all of the T.A. High students are within about a 10-year age span and it is this group who attend these reunions. I attended the first one in 1980 and others in 2000, 2005, 2010 and 2013. There were sure a lot of old people there. I missed the last one in about 2021.

Of course there were lots of pretty town girls but I was pretty shy and didn't try to compete with the town boys for their attention. Why would a town girl want anything to do with a country bumpkin? And besides, I had to take a bus the 20 miles home every day so what chance would I have of even thinking of dating. I found out many years later that more than one of them had a crush on me...rats!! too soon old and too late smart.

I remember a couple of embarrassing situations when I was in Grade ten...horrors—this farm kid who already felt like a country bumpkin. I never mastered swimming beyond the dog paddle stage but we used to bike down to the river to "swim" or at least splash around.

One day I took Gavin with me (I think he was about 6 and I was about 16). When we were ready to head for home I didn't want to waste time fully dressing him so I just shoved his undershorts in my pocket. In those days we usually carried a handkerchief around in our pocket and the next day in school I felt my nose ready to drip so I whipped out my hanky...but it wasn't a hanky. It went back in my pocket in a hurry...I doubt anyone saw what had happened but I was sick with embarrassment.

The Farm Kid And The Flying Bank

It was popular in those days to wear a V-neck sweater over your shirt. This situation happened in the winter so I was also wearing long johns. I had a shirt that I liked but the elbows were completely worn out and my underwear was quite visible.

However, the long sleeved V-neck covered all but the collar and cuffs of the shirt so no problem. When I arrived at school I took off my winter jacket to hang it up and, to my utter horror, I had forgotten to put the V neck on. What to do—well I rolled up my sleeves as high as I could with the underwear sleeves rolled up underneath the shirt sleeves and had to endure the day with what looked like Popeye muscles.

I'm sure I got some curious stares, especially when nobody else even rolled up their sleeves, but I don't remember anyone mocking me. I dressed much more carefully after that.

When I was in Grade 11 my great uncle Ed Brown (My Grandpa's brother) and Aunt Edna moved to a small house near the home of his sister Edna (Ab & Edna Owen) near the river.

Uncle Ed had a couple of milk cows and one winter he took sick so I was asked to stay with them so I could milk the cows and do chores. Uncle Ed was a prince of a man and everyone who knew him loved him.

Anyway, one evening he was suffering chest pains and I can remember him laying on his stomach and holding a cushion to his chest which apparently eased the pain somewhat.

My Great Uncle Mill Brown (another of Grandpa's brothers) lived in Nampa where he ran the General Store. He had a car so he was quickly summoned to drive Uncle Ed to the hospital. The next morning when I woke up there was nobody in the house but I had to go to school so I went ahead and did the milking, then walked up to Uncle Ab and Aunt Edna's house.

Aunt Edna Brown was there along with other family members and I was informed that Uncle Ed had passed away. He was only 60. I think I skipped school that day.

I started driving our car around home when I was about 12 or 13, even earlier sitting between dad's legs and just steering. However, I was almost 18 and part way through Grade 12 before I got a Drivers' license so that kind of limited any dating opportunities.

The Farm Kid And The Flying Bank

However, Dad had bought an old pickup truck from Jay, and Jay had bought it, I think, in the Edmonton area. It was a 1942 Chev that had been repainted in two tone green with lots of extra bumper guards and chrome things added to it so it was kind of unique and a bit gaudy but not totally unattractive.

By this time I had a bit of a crush on a gal in Grade 11 who rode the school bus from Reno. Her name was Annie Lebedinski....a nice girl and pretty good looking. Anyway, dad actually let me take the truck to pick Annie up at her home and go to a school dance in Peace River.

I remember her mom talking a lot in Ukrainian when I picked her up and had no idea what she was saying...but I expect she was warning Annie about all those things young girls are warned about. A school bus had also been arranged to bus kids from the area to the dance and apparently the bus driver spent his waiting time in Peace River at one of the bars.

It rained quite a lot that evening and on the way home on the Reno road the bus tried to pass me. As he was about even with me the back of the bus skidded towards the ditch and his front bumper swung around and knocked me into the opposite ditch leaving a pretty good dent in my back fender. There were 8 or 10 kids on the bus so they all bailed out and pushed me out of the ditch. Then they jumped into the back of my truck and I drove them home, leaving the bus driver to his own devices. I`m not sure why but I guess dad believed me as to what had happened as he never even gave me hell when he saw the bent up fender.

Dances at the Nampa Hall were a fairly regular occurrence when I was a teenager. One day Uncle Cliff mentioned that he would like to go to the Halloween Masquerade dance and somebody, not sure who, suggested that I dress up as a girl and go as his date. I think I was about 16. Mom did a good job of dressing me up, with a bandanna on my head and curlers in the front, a dress, a bosom, et al.

I don`t really remember much about the dance but the next day a neighbor ran into dad and mentioned that he had seen Val at the dance. Needless to say, Val was fit to be tied. I wasn`t real happy about it either...imagine somebody thinking I looked like Val!!!

For a number of years Dad was the local weed inspector. In addition to making farm inspections it was his responsibility to hire somebody to cut and treat noxious weeds along the public roadways. So for two years in a row he hired a neighbor, Harry Hazel, and me.

The first year I made $1.an hour and the second year I got a raise to $1.10 an hour. We would cut the weeds, mainly sow thistle and Canada thistle, with a scythe. Then stack them and burn them, and treat the ground with a chemical called `sodium chlorate` which sterilized the ground for up to seven years. I expect that chemical is now banned.

But ah...I had another source of income...besides selling pop bottles and the odd squirrel hide. We usually had two or three sows in the old barn...well it wasn`t that old but it never got a proper roof so leaked quite a bit.

It was my job to feed the hogs and milk a couple of cows and this job fell solely on me when dad was away in the winter. It was a crappy job...cutting holes in the ice from the new dugout and hauling it to the pigs and cows, doing all this in the dark before I left for school and after I got home. But dad was fair about it...I got to keep and sell one pig from every litter. This amounted to about $20. a hog about 4 times a year.

I don't think dad ever found out but I almost always lost the works playing poker on the school bus. I just wasn`t a very good poker player...but I learned a bit about the game.

I once was helping Uncle Cliff load an old sow that he was shipping to market. He had the sow in the old barn and opened the sliding barn door just wide enough to accommodate the loading chute. His old International truck was fixed with side boards and a gate at the back.

The truck was backed up to the "high" end of the chute and it was my job to slam the gate down as soon as the sow was in. It took Uncle Cliff forever to persuade the old sow to head up the chute and the air was truly blue. But finally.... she headed up the chute on the run—just as the old truck slowly rolled away from the chute. She hit the ground on the fly and, needless to say, she wasn't shipped that day—and Uncle Cliff was not pleased.

The summer I graduated I worked for Steve Petluk (he's the guy who married Doris Owen...remember...my grade one teacher with the ruler.) It mostly involved driving a tractor doing field work and most often 10 or 12 hours a day or more. He paid me the grand sum of $100. a month plus room and board when I required it.

I must have been a good farm hand because when I got a job with the bank he tried to persuade me to stay.

Hells bells...I could make $129. a month at the Bank.

7
DONE WITH SCHOOL

In High School, I chose the "academic" program rather than the "business" program, and graduated in June 1959 with over 100 credits and my high school diploma. Dad said he could cover up to two years of university, and it was my plan to become a school teacher...that was one professional job that only required two years of university at that time.

However, I didn't do very well in Social Studies and French, so I was a little short of meeting the University entrance requirements. I did like math and science and did well in those subjects but took some of the other courses a bit too casually.

A number of my friends who took the "business program" had received invitations from local Banks to apply for a job…they were looking for career bankers. I did not receive an invitation, but walked into the old "Canadian Bank of Commerce" in Peace River one day and applied for a job.

The Farm Kid And The Flying Bank

I had no trouble getting hired and my plan was to work for one year while taking French and Social Studies by correspondence and applying for University once I had those courses.

Well, I enrolled in the correspondence courses, and I think I actually submitted a lesson or two. However, with a little jingle in my pockets (and I do mean "little"), I discovered there could be more to life than working and then going home every night.

Needless to say, 38 years later, I retired from the Bank...which had amalgamated with the Imperial Bank of Canada in 1961 and was now the 'Canadian Imperial Bank of Commerce'...and is still known as CIBC.

My starting salary was $1,850. annually, but because Peace River was considered a northern branch, I also got another $400. annually as a living allowance. The princely sum of $187.50 a month, less taxes. I believe I netted $64.50 every payday...twice a month.

I was to start work on September 1st, which also happened to be the first day of school that year. As Dad was busy harvesting, he said he couldn't drive me to work, so I did the logical thing.

I caught the school bus to Peace River. I'm sure the driver and some of the kids wondered why I was wearing a tie and my white Sports coat (the one my folks had bought for my Grade 12 Graduation), but it got me there. I think I got a ride home with a neighbor, June Williams, who worked in the Post Office in Peace River, and I think I rode to work and back with her for awhile.

At any rate, I eventually rented a basement suite jointly with a young Post Office employee...likely arranged through June. Eddie was a different kind of a guy....looking back, I think he may have been gay, but at that time I honestly didn't know that gay people existed.

Eddie had made a big stack of "mail boxes" out of cardboard, together with a bunch of cards, about letter size, with town names written on them. Then he would spend the best part of each evening practicing his sorting skills. I usually went out and left him alone with his sorting. It wasn't long after we moved into the basement suite that the Post Office transferred Eddie out, and I could not afford the place on my own.

That's when I either advertised for a roommate or found an ad in the local paper where another fellow was looking for someone to share the rent. In any event...that's how I met a guy by the name of Al Anderson...an 18-year-old DJ at the new radio station. We hit it off from the get-go and did a lot of partying together.

He also had a nice 1955 Ford Crown Victoria two-door car (baby blue and chrome) that he let me borrow from time to time. He was dating Lynda McArthur, who had been in the same class as my sister Val, so I kind of knew her from school.

Al had to work the early morning shift, so he often went to bed reasonably early...that's when I used his car to date a girl named Ruth Weins. I never put a scratch on the car, but had some close calls with it, which I finally told Al about a few years ago.

My first job in the Bank was as a "collection clerk." This involved several tasks which have long since been eliminated from bank duties or totally computerized so I won't go into all that.

After a few months, I worked in the Current Account Department using mechanical posting machines...which I never did master. Then I was transferred to a teller's position and taught how to run cash by "Mary",...a gal who had been with the bank for some time and actually used a ruler to rap my knuckles if I screwed up rolling coins or counting bills the wrong way.

In those days, all tellers operated in a cage with a locking door at the back, and I was responsible for the key. I also had a gun, which all tellers had to have in those days. Although it sat in front of me just below my cash drawer, I was warned never to touch it. It wouldn't have worked anyway, as it was in several pieces. Apparently, the bonding or insurance coverage required that we be armed in the event of a robbery.

I had to wear a suit or sports coat and tie in the bank, and had none other than the White Sports Coat. I went to the Sears office to see if I could buy a suit on time, but as I was only 18, they needed my dad to co-sign for me. My dad flatly refused, so I had no choice but to wear that white sports coat until I had saved up the $29.95 (or whatever it was) so I could buy a suit.

One of my High school buddies, Walter Romaniuk, had a car that he wanted to sell to me, and I really wanted to buy it...my first set of wheels. It was a 1948 Mercury coupe, maroon coloured, and he was asking $400. He agreed to accept four payments of $100. So I gave him 4 post-dated cheques.

The age of majority at that time was 21, so he had my mom sign each cheque with me. I don't know if that would have helped or not. I have no idea how I managed to handle the car payments along with rent, etc., but those cheques were all covered.

1948 Mercury Coupe..just like my first car

Shortly after I had bought the Mercury, my sister Lynne wanted to go to a dance at Nampa. She was about 14 at the time. Mom relented to let her go, but only if she went with me as a chaperone. Well…I think she had a good time, and so did I.

I ran into some old school buddies who were well equipped with lemon gin, and I got myself pretty well bent out of shape. About all I remember is driving home with my head out the window, puking my guts out while Lynne leaned over and steered.

Thankfully, we didn't run into any cops…I was well under aged. Lynne kept her mouth shut, and we didn't tell Mom about this episode until many years later.

In June of 1960, I received my first transfer…to Chetwynd, B.C. I had no idea where Chetwynd was, but learned it was about 65 miles west of Dawson Creek, B.C.

Looking back, I think I could have collected a few dollars for mileage (for which I think they paid .10¢ a mile) to at least cover the cost of Al's gas, but I don't remember even knowing that was available. Chetwynd was pretty much a lumber town with two large mills in town and not far from the Indigenous Reserve on Moberly Lake.

The local bar was pretty rough, although I left Chetwynd before I was old enough to frequent it. Likely just as well. Chetwynd was also a rail hub for Pacific Great Eastern (PGE), with the line coming from the west through the mountains and then splitting in Chetwynd, with one line going northeast to Fort St. John and the other East to Dawson Creek.

The Farm Kid And The Flying Bank

A search of the internet reveals these notes: After World War I PGE was bought by the Government of British Columbia and in 1972 the name of the railway was finally changed to British Columbia Railway (B.C. Railway.) "The Chetwynd Yard includes a passing track, four classification tracks, two diesel servicing tracks, a rip track, a trailer ramp, and the station and freight shed. There is also a small mechanical shop and fuel pump house next to the servicing tracks."

Because of all the rail activity, there were a lot of railway employees in town, most of whom were Europeans living in bunkhouse-style accommodation.

As I recall, they were mostly from Portugal and Italy. They used to send most of their earnings "back home" to their families and lived as cheaply as they could, and I think they must have lived on bread and garlic sausage.

The Chetwynd branch of the Bank was very small...likely room for no more than about 6 or 8 customers comfortably at a time. Anyway, on PGE payday, they would crowd into the bank and on hot summer days, the stench of sweat and garlic was positively overwhelming.

I can't remember why, but I didn't take my car to Chetwynd until several months later...Perhaps I couldn't afford the insurance, although it probably wasn't very much.

Al and Lynda drove me to Chetwynd, and Ruth went along, and we had a tearful departure. Her tears...not mine. I was the "teller-accountant", which meant nothing more than a glorified teller...But I learned to do lots of things that the average teller, in those days at least, was not expected to do. I had a handgun here also...which I was warned not to touch.

Chetwynd was actually a sub-branch of Dawson Creek, B.C., and Bert Lachman was the "Officer in Charge." I think he had a lending limit of $300. above which, he needed the approval of the Dawson Creek manager (Mr. Kurt Alfke). Alice was an English lady who posted all the ledgers by hand... We were one of the last branches in the country to receive a mechanical posting machine. We did have one or two old-fashioned calculators, but I usually added up my cash sheet at the end of the day by hand. I was pretty good with numbers.

Bert and I shared a small bank-owned house behind the bank, and I think I paid about $23 a month for my share of the rent. We had no plumbing, but an outdoor privy with two holes. Why two holes??? That was customary - even our outhouse back at Nampa had two...But I don't ever remember sharing the privacy with anyone else.

Anyway, one weekend when Bert was gone, several buddies came in for some partying. I thought I had the place pretty well cleaned up before I hit the sack, but Bert arrived home about 1 AM and booted me out of bed to clean the outhouse.

Unknown to me, one of my "friends" had been drinking vodka and orange juice and had puked all over the toilet seat. Being winter, it was frozen on good so there I was in the middle of the night scraping and cleaning up this stuff.

I spent about two years in Chetwynd and earned a little extra income working at the local theatre...selling tickets or popcorn, ushering, and on occasion even running the projectors. I worked there with a very attractive blond gal named Sheila, but one of my friends, Doug, was dating her, so I never asked her out.

One time when we where double dating...I dated another girl for awhile (cannot remember her name). Sheila said, "I chased Dennis for 6 months, but he never caught on." Curses...still a slow dumb farm kid.

I would often hitch a ride into Dawson Creek, sometimes with Bert and sometimes not, where a banking friend by the name of Al Higginson worked, and I would catch a ride home with him.

Actually, he lived in Berwyn, so my folks would meet me there and take me home for the weekend. Sometime during the first year in Chetwynd, I brought my 48 Mercury back with me, but couldn't afford to drive it much.

Then the radiator sprung a leak which I couldn't afford to fix so I finally listed it for sale. I sold it to an Indigenous fellow for $125. but he only had $100. and promised to bring in the other $25. on "Monday" when he supposedly got paid.

Well, that Monday never arrived. However, I did run into him in Dawson Creek some time later and hit him up for the money. Yes, yes...he just had to call his boss to get his cheque so he could pay me...but could I lend him $2. for the phone call? Never saw him again, so I was out another $2.

Sometime after that, while I was back in Peace River on vacation, Dad agreed to co-sign for me to buy a 1959 Ford car. It was a cheaper custom model 300 but it was wheels and not too old...it had been a rental car.

I believe I paid $1,300. for it with payments to Traders Finance of $64. a month. When I got that baby back to Chetwynd, I suddenly had many carless friends. If that car could talk.....I had a cop stop me once, and he thoroughly searched my car and remarked that rumours were that I was drinking a lot and had better cool it.

I did get quite tipsy a couple of times, but I really didn't drink that often. The one time I over did it was in the presence of a local storekeeper that gave this information to the cop because he made his daughter break up with me after observing my inebriated performance at a local dance. (and that was the cute girl whose name escapes me).

A 1959 Ford Custom 300 like the one I had (same colour)

Now with a newer car, I made more trips home to Nampa and Peace River for weekends. I was always broke so I would gas up at the local gas station where the owner knew me. I would write a cheque for an extra $10. which was my spending money for the weekend.

Before I left Peace River, I would go to the local dry cleaners where the owner knew me from my days in the bank there and cash a cheque large enough to cover the one I had written in Chetwynd.

As out-of-town cheques in those days took a few days to clear, my pay would go through in time to cover the Peace River cheque. I thought this was a pretty neat way to finance my trips until I found out that it was actually "kiting" and totally illegal. I had to quit that practice before I got found out and canned.

During the latter time of my stay in Chetwynd, I dated an indigenous girl named Elizabeth (Liz) Paquette. She was actually a very nice girl, who lived with her parents at the Moberly Lake reserve, and I enjoyed visiting their home and they were always very kind to me.

One weekend, they even agreed to let Liz go home to Nampa with me to meet my parents...BUT....as long as I took her younger sister (about 10 years old) with me. So I did. When I left Chetwynd, I left Liz behind, and that was the end of that relationship, except one day I got a letter from her telling me how much she missed me and all that good stuff. However, as it happens, I was already married by then, so that didn't go over too well with you know who.

During my time in Chetwynd, I was asked to stand up for my buddy Al Anderson as he and Lynda were getting married. That would have been in July 1961. One of Al's friends, who I ran into at either the reception or the bachelor party, asked to borrow my car to run up town for some more beer or cigarettes or who knows what. Although I didn't know the guy, he was apparently a friend of Al's so, no problem. Well...it was a problem.

He brought the car back with one of the front fenders pretty well crumpled, but told me that the other guy's insurance would cover it. Shortly after that, I went to the police station to find out who the other party was and was told that my car was at fault and "good luck, Charlie." As I couldn't afford to get it fixed, I drove it like that until I traded it off.

In April of 1962, I was transferred to Dawson Creek as a Current Account supervisor. This time, I was aware of, and collected, mileage. All my worldly possessions fit into my car, so I collected .10¢ / mile for the 65-mile drive—a whole $6.50.

My job was to oversee the posting and balancing of all ledgers and statements on the mechanical posting machines. The ledger was yellow paper, and the statement (which eventually went to the customer) was white. It meant posting all cheques and deposits twice...by two different people, and they had to balance with each other at the end of the day. They seldom did, and then began the "cross-check" to find what had gone wrong. All postings were copied on long sheets of paper, and these had to be thoroughly gone over and compared with each other until the error was found and corrected.

Quite frankly, I had no idea what I was doing, having never really run one of the machines on my own. (Remember my training on these machines in Peace River?) Fortunately, the girls in that department were pretty experienced, and they had pity on me and tolerated my ignorance even though I was their supervisor.

Fortunately, that job only lasted a couple of months before I was transferred to Whitecourt, Alberta.

8
SINGLE LIFE OVER...

I reported for work at Whitecourt about mid-June 1962 as the branch Accountant. (a title which has long since disappeared from the banking business). I was essentially in charge of the tellers and ledger keepers and even acted in the Manager's place in his absence. This branch had been a former "Imperial Bank of Canada" and, at amalgamation one year earlier, everything was to have been changed to the new forms styled after the Canadian Bank of Commerce forms. Nothing much had been done in that regard, so we had a big job on our hands. It was a good learning experience.

The Manager at that time was Eli Stasyk who later was transferred to Jamaica and I have no idea where he went after that. We had a staff of about 8 or 9, including two male tellers, Gary & Darryl. Darryl left the Bank while I was there and went to work in the oil business and Gary did the same shortly after I left Whitecourt.

I often wished I had done that also. I can't remember the names of other staff other than "Polly

Konzuk", who was a character. Mr. Stasyk once talked to her about keeping her voice down when there were customers in the office…she one time shouted across the office to a customer, telling him his account was overdrawn. I'm sure the customer appreciated other customers knowing that.

Anyway, Polly came to work the next day with a black arm band…her explanation was that if this place was going to be as quiet as a morgue, she may as well dress for it. We had a customer who came in every so often to have us send a bank draft overseas payable to a "Knut Hansen." When I checked the entries at the end of each day…pardon my blushing…she had always typed "Kunt Hansen."

There were single men's living quarters at the rear of the Bank, which consisted of not much more than two bedrooms, a bathroom, and a sink, a hotplate and a few dishes, as I recall. But the price was right. Gary & I lived there for awhile.

Gary was from the Camrose area and had a girlfriend there by the name of Sandra, and he called her almost every night from one of the phones in the office. I had given him a hard time about what he could possibly talk about every night, especially when he drove home to Camrose almost every weekend. He assured me that it was just mostly idle chit chat and suggested one evening that I pick up one of the other phones and listen in. So I did...After a brief salutation, Sandra said, "Gary.....I'm pregnant." I quietly hung up the phone and left him alone for the rest of the call.

The local telephone office was the second building over from the Bank, and in the evenings I sometimes talked to the various telephone operators ...and did this for a while before actually meeting any of them.

It got so I spent more time talking to a Peggy Duncan than the others and she finally agreed to meet me…I think she actually invited me to the office as she was working alone.

In any event, sparks eventually flew, and we began dating…Remember I had this 1959 Ford car…still with a crumpled fender. Gary worked in the evenings at the local drive-in theatre, and he would let us in for free...and I would usually buy burgers and pop.

Peggy still accuses me of having often borrowed money from her for our treats...then pocketing the change. I don't remember doing this but, if I did, it was certainly unintentional. Why didn't she say something then???

Gary and Sandra were married late that summer but, in the meantime, he and I had moved into Polly Konzuk's basement suite, which was a little better equipped. When he found out that I was engaged, we had to decide who would stay in the suite and who would have to seek housing elsewhere. We simply flipped a coin...and I won. Gary and Sandra wound up renting a kitchenette by the month in one of the local motels.

Peggy and one or more of her friends were going to the Pentecostal Church...which I found to be very evangelical with weird ideas...talking in tongues and that kind of thing.

Anyway, she wanted me to accept Jesus as my personal saviour....so, one night while parking somewhere, I told her I had done so. That seemed to make her happy, and the dating thing went pretty well after that. The truth is...I just wanted to win her over.

One day a salesman for Peoples Jewellers came to the bank to see me...he said he had been sent over by Mrs. Duncan to sell me an engagement ring. Well...I wasn't really thinking very seriously about getting married for awhile, at least, but...what the heck. I had no money, but I think the ring was about $100. and they carried the financing at $10. a month. I gave her the ring on Halloween day that same year.

Our wedding day, December 8, 1962. Back row: Larry (Butch) Duncan – Peggy's brother, Gavin, Leona Wolfe, Bob Good. Front: Lynne, Edwin Talbot, Peg and me. Leona was a friend of Peggy's and Bob Good a friend of mine from Chetwynd. I haven't seen or had any contact with him since that day. We did see Leona and her husband when we were in Dawson Creek in the late 60's but not since.

We got married in the Pentecostal Church on Dec. 8, 1962 and may have attended Church a few times after that but I was not at all comfortable there and we both left the Pentecostal Church behind not long after we were married. The church apparently didn't believe in dancing, so we never had a wedding dance...much to the disappointment of many of my relatives.

Why on earth did we get married in December...when we didn't have to...really! Well, in those days, at least you could claim your wife as a full year's exemption if you were married by December 31st. and the tax savings was well worth it. I think I got back about $85.

That winter we spent pretty much every weekend with Gary & Sandra playing rummoli...sometimes all night. Then we would often cook bacon and eggs before the visiting couple went home. We got paid twice a month, and Gary and I would take turns buying a case of beer for the weekend...I think a dozen beer was under $5.00 in those days. The Pentecostal church would have frowned on that. The girls looked after our jar of pennies that we needed for rummoli and after a full winter of playing one of us was up a dollar at the most.

I was always broke, but thought with Peggy working at the telephone office, we would be in much better shape. Alas, it wasn't long before she found out she was pregnant and had to quit work so there went all that extra income.

The Farm Kid And The Flying Bank

In fact, we put the car up on blocks that winter
to save money. Before our baby was born, we
moved from the basement suite into a small house,
which we rented—I think we paid about $85. a
month...a princely sum when I was only clearing
about $200. a month.

It was a little two-room house, and we had an
old china cabinet thing that we used to separate the
"kitchen" from the "living room." The owners had
used half of the bedroom closet to install an actual
flushing toilet, although no room for a tub or sink.
In fact, we pretty much had to back into it. Because
I needed a place to shave in the mornings, I
installed a little shelf in the closet in front of the
toilet, with a basin of water for shaving. It was
propped up with a board so it could be folded out of
the way…likely my first attempt at carpentry. Once
in a while, we would use the toilet without folding
the shelf down and then absentmindedly stand up
and dump the basin over ourselves.

Jean Louise was born the following September
19th. (1963) and, as there was no hospital in
Whitecourt at that time, it was about a 25-mile drive
to Mayerthorpe. Peggy was timing her contractions
with a big old wind-up alarm clock we took in the
car with us, and we made it safely. Peggy did go

back to work at the telephone office after a bit, working nights, so I could babysit. She was afraid that I wouldn't hear Jeannie wake up, so we got a long cord for our phone and hung the phone over the head of our bed. She would listen in from the telephone office every once in awhile and if she heard anything, she would yell as loud as she could to wake me up.

I guess I was already awake one night when Jeannie projectile vomited…like a geyser…right up and over the bassinette she was in. I also remember putting a bottle of milk in a pan on the stove to warm it up.

I went back to sleep and awoke only after the pot had boiled dry…as did the baby bottle, with milk all over the stove and the ceiling. That might have been quite a geyser also…sorry I missed it.

9

OUR LITTLE FAMILY MAKES A BIG MOVE

One day in 1963, a letter arrived at the Bank from the Regional Office addressed to me personally. I had been transferred to the branch at 8536- 109th. Street, Edmonton, as Branch Accountant. The Manager was Bill Sorobey. That branch no longer exists, but at that time, it was considered the University Branch, and we had a lot of accounts for Professors and Doctors and tons of students. In fact, I was working at that branch when Canada Student Loans were introduced so it was a very busy office.

We found an older home to rent on about 86th. Ave. South and 97 St., not all that far from work. This time, I was given a reasonable moving allowance, and my boyhood friend Peter Cruickshank (mentioned above, Chapter 6) was by this time operating a small trucking company in Edmonton. I hired him to move our belongings (which didn't amount to a lot), but it helped him out.

Peter was an avid photographer and set up a dark room in our basement and was a frequent guest at our place. Consequently, we have many great black and white pictures of that era...mostly of Jeannie, who was a year or two old and, apparently, one of his favorite subjects.

As a matter of fact, Peter's love for photography eventually led to his establishing several photo developing outlets in Edmonton and surrounding towns. He was there when photography moved into the digital age, and he told me he had just invested in a lot of expensive equipment for the "new age" not long before he was diagnosed with cancer.

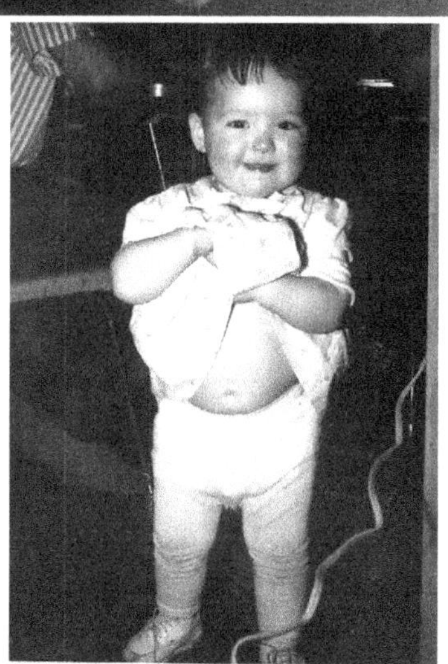

Some photos of Jeannie as taken by Peter and developed in his dark room in our basement.

I don't think that car seat would meet today's legal requirements. It simply hung over the seat back, and in this photo, it is hung on the outside of the car door to keep her in check while we were picnicking.

One day, I was heading over to Uncle Alex's with Jeannie in the car seat beside me—I can't remember why Peggy wasn't with me. Anyway, the route to the west end included travelling the Groat Road, which is a pretty twisty road.

Going around one of the corners, Jeannie slipped out of the car seat onto the floor on the passenger side. Of course I couldn't stop until I got to the end of Groat Road and found someplace to pull over so I had to let her lay there while she screamed her head off. She was not hurt and I don't think she holds that against me.

I was now authorized to handle and carry one of the branch handguns, which I would stick in my suit pocket, with the grip sticking out, whenever we had to go to the main branch to pick up a cash supply. Of course I had a permit to carry the gun, as I did at subsequent branches, but it could not be concealed. At all rural branches and some city branches, prior to 1972, the cash parcel would arrive at the Post Office and two people (one armed) would have to sign for it and take it back to the branch. I often went along as the "unarmed" employee.

One day, I drove to the main branch alone to pick up cash and, as the gun was uncomfortable in my pocket, I laid it on the passenger seat. (yes that was against the rules but we had no option that day.)

On the way back to the branch, some jerk passed me and jammed on his brakes and gave me the one-finger salute...I guess he thought I had cut him off, but I don't think I did. He seemed almost threatening (yep...road rage in those days too), and I thought quite seriously of just showing him the gun, but thankfully better discretion prevailed.

Lory was born at the old Misericordia Hospital in Edmonton on July 15, 1965. We were now a family of four.

While in Edmonton, I felt that we needed a newer car but couldn't really afford much so decided to look at a smaller car—compact cars were just starting to make their appearance in the marketplace. So we went shopping....and ended up trading the 1959 Ford in on a used 1965 Rambler American. It was definitely smaller but served us well for several years. I can't remember what I paid for the car but I know I received only $300. for the trade-in and the damned salesman referred to it as "a junker" – it still had the banged-in fender. Uncle Alex, who was living in Edmonton then, used to tease me about my junker almost every time I saw him.

Uncle Alex and Aunt Millie McConnell had by this time sold their farm at Nampa and moved to Edmonton, where Uncle Alex worked as a school custodian (Janitor), and Ian and Sheena finished their schooling there.

Ian was always interested in mechanics, worked in a garage, and was married to Darlene. Their first son, Shane, was born about the same time as Lory. Also, my cousin Lorne Day, who was a few years younger than me but had married when he was only about 17, to Bonnie, was also living in Edmonton at that time. So we spent a lot of time with all of them and took the Rambler American on a holiday to the Okanogan with Lorne & Bonnie.

I built a large plywood box to strap to the top of the car, which was filled with our tent and camping gear, and away we went…the first time any of us had seen the Rocky Mountains. We covered a lot of ground…camping in Penticton…renting a cabin at Ainsworth Hot Springs on Kootenay Lake, and even crossing the border to go to Oroville,

Washington...the first time any of us had been to the US.

All of us but Lorne were old enough to go to the bar there, so we decided to "have a beer in the USA." The bartender never even questioned Lorne, but wanted I.D. from Peggy, which she did not have on her. We suggested she sit in the car and wait for us but she didn't go for that, so we didn't get our US beer until many years later.

Our venture even included a trip to Peace River and Nampa to visit my folks and Lorne's mother, who was living in Peace River at that time. The box on top was likely much heavier than it should have been, as the drive shaft would rub on the floorboards every time we hit a dip in the road. But....it got us safely home.

The back seat was not very big, but Peggy and Bonnie endured the trip without a lot of complaining. They did complain, though, when Lorne and I chose to pitch the tent in Penticton right next to one with three single girls in it. Honestly, we didn't know it was a girls' only tent...honest.

Several years later, Lorne & Bonnie moved to Whitecourt with their family, and that is where

Bonnie succumbed to lung cancer at the early age of 42.

Ian and Darlene had two boys (Shane and Jamie), and they, along with Sheena, followed Uncle Alex & Aunt Millie to the west coast, where Ian worked as a supervisor in a Vehicle Inspection station. Sheena worked in a dental office and married Dale Sharp, a professional artist and a great guy. Ian and Darlene subsequently divorced; Ian remarried (to Vi) and had two more children, Mathew & Shannon.

Ian committed suicide in 1985. A blow to all of us, and we never knew why it happened.

10
ON THE MOVE AGAIN

In late 1965, I received another personal letter from the Bank's Regional Office directing me to report to the Beaverlodge, Alberta branch as Branch Accountant. I think it may have been my first move after the Bank had substantially enhanced our moving package, and it now included a "rug and drape" allowance. Peggy was telling my mom about this and said, "Now we even get a Drug and Rape allowance." My mom's comment was, "Well, that's nice."

We enjoyed Beaverlodge and rented a fairly large but older home from one of the more prominent businessmen in town. The house was on two lots so we had a huge yard, and even though it was on the Town's main street, only a block or two from the branch, the yard was completely hidden from view with great shrubs and trees. It was a great place to raise two little kids. Living in Beaverlodge meant we were much closer to my folks at Nampa.

Sometime during my stay in Beaverlodge, the old Bank building was replaced with the new building at the same location, as it was a prime corner downtown. The plan was to jack up the old building and skid it to the rear of the lot from which we would operate until the new office opened. Well we arrived for work one cold Monday in November to find the old building moved, on large skids about 4 feet off the ground.

The original vault had not been moved...well nigh impossible I expect. It stood alone and apart from the bank building, with the vault door about three or four feet above ground level as well. It had a couple of boards on two sawhorses in front of it, with a step ladder for us to climb up on.

Of course we had to remove a lot of stuff, including cash, from the vault so we could operate the branch. Security was provided by the local RCMP for this operation but we found out that we first had to hold a space heater close to the combination dials before they would turn.

The old building on skids had a makeshift step in front so customers and staff could get in and out, but we had no plumbing or heat. We did have power, so we had to round up a number of little space heaters and place one at each station. The staff all worked in winter garb, removing their gloves only long enough to count cash. Our pens had to be warmed up in front of the space heaters before they would write.

Fortunately, heat was restored within a couple of days but we had the "outside" vault for the remainder of the winter. Once the new building was completed, with a new vault, everything was transferred (with lots of RCMP security) and the old vault was then jackhammered down...a process taking many days.

Moving the old Beaverlodge Branch – new one in background – and the Grand opening.

Grand Opening photos of the new Beaverlodge office. That is Mr. "G" (on the right) and Basil Langveldt, then the Alberta Superintendent, in the doorway.

I spent about two years in Beaverlodge and most of the time under the management of Mr. "G" (name withheld). Several months before I left Beaverlodge Mr. "G" began acting very strange and he was soon put on extended medical leave. It was a strange and worrisome environment to work in for awhile but thankfully one or more of our customers realized something wasn't right and recognizing that I was in a difficult position they called the Regional Office in Calgary.

Of course this meant a swift visit by Bank Auditors and I learned after the fact that they thought they would be coming in to fire several of us and bring in some people to run the branch until a new Manager could be appointed.

After finding nothing wrong as far as a branch audit was concerned and realizing that I was actually capably dealing with a lot of the lending business, they decided they could leave the branch in my charge for a few weeks until a new Manager was found.

Before the above turn of events Mr. "G" was busy with a customer in his office one day and it was getting close to closing time on a Friday night.

A fellow came into the branch and wanted to see the Manager. I could tell that he had been drinking and I was sure the Manager didn't want to see him so I offered to help. What he wanted was a loan of $5. as his wife desperately needed a medical prescription and he was short of cash. I started by telling him that the Bank didn't make $5.00 loans to which he replied "Then give me $50.)

Although I knew that I likely wouldn't be able to accommodate him I began by asking him if he had anything for security to which he offered his saddle which I tactfully declined.

Then I asked him if he knew anyone who might co-sign for him and his answer was, "Oh sure…Mr. Inkster at the Hardware store in Hythe (about 8 miles away) has lent me money many times so I am sure he will sign for me."

My answer to that was "well, why don't you borrow from Mr. Inkster now?" His reply, "Because I am on foot and by the time I get back the liquor store will be closed"

In 1967 Mom and Dad agreed to look after Jeannie and Lory and we booked a trip via train to Montreal for Expo '67. By far the furthest we had ever been from home and I am pretty sure I borrowed the money from the Bank but it was a great experience and, for the most part at least, we enjoyed the train ride.

The line ups at Expo were ridiculous but that was the way it was and we went with the flow. On the train we met another young couple from Grande Prairie and we spent a fair bit of time with them. For all but one day the heat and humidity was almost unbearably high.

Our friends were very religious so - every once in awhile we would accidently lose them at Expo so we could go to a beer tent. We also managed to fit in a night or two in Toronto and a trip to Niagara Falls while we were there.

Not long after we returned from that trip I received a letter inviting me to spend a week (or was it two?) at the Bank's staff college in Toronto. As I recall we drove to Edmonton where Peggy and the kids stayed with my sister Lynne and her then husband Ernie and I had my very first plane ride...on a jet no less.

The Bank's college in those days was a building that was known as the Eaton house and was apparently the home of Timothy Eaton at one time, and later a home for unwed mothers. It was a huge structure with spacious and beautiful grounds.

It was quite a facility with several bedrooms, classrooms, and bathrooms and a good kitchen and dining room.

Some evenings, a group of us would take a cab to downtown Toronto to enjoy the nightlife, fine restaurants, Stripper clubs, et al....a real eye-opening deal for this farm kid. Over the following years, I wound up having several trips to the college...most recently as an Area Manager in about 1987.

Actually, one of the instructors at one of the courses I attended there later became a fellow Area Manager working out of Calgary as I did...I had rural branches; he had smaller city branches.

11
ANOTHER MOVE

In the fall of 1967, another personal letter arrived from the Regional Office with instructions to report to the Ponoka, Alberta, branch as Branch Accountant. This was a considerably larger branch and was a good promotion. The Manager was Ken Wolstenholme, who was a great fellow not far from retirement and he made sure that I got quite involved in the lending business, even though that was not part of my position description. It was great training for me and certainly gave me a jump start for my ensuing transfer that did involve lending.

Shortly after arriving in Ponoka, the Manager got a call from the Bank's Human Resources Department asking if I would consider a move to Fort McMurray as Branch Manager. The idea sounded exciting...a Branch Manager no less, even if it did have only 5 or 6 on staff. But, after discussing the pros and cons at length with Mr. Wolstenholme, he convinced me that it would not be in my best interest. He pointed out that it was about 300 miles from Edmonton on a gravel road and a pretty rough town and why would I want to take my family up there?

I can't remember who went up there instead, but I do remember that within about 3 years, the branch ballooned to 25 or 30 on staff and he got at least two or three promotions as the town boomed and the branch grew rapidly. Perhaps I should have gone.

We spent about two years in Ponoka and our family of four rented the apartment above the Bank...I think the rent was $43. a month... It was fairly large but was somewhat like living in a hotel with several bedrooms and a large front "sitting room area."

The branch was built in the early 1900's and the upstairs was originally built as living quarters for male staff. We had lots of room and the rent was cheap but we had no yard. A door opened onto a flat roof that was basically tar and gravel and this was our kids' play area. They would have been about two and four when we moved there.

The second story of the building provided walls on three sides of their "play area" but on the street side the "wall" was only about a foot tall so of course, we couldn't let the kids out there by themselves. One of us would usually sit on the "wall" to make sure they didn't venture too close lest they fall onto a pedestrian on the street below.

Whenever there was a change in supervisory staff, the combination numbers on the vault and the safes within had to be changed. Every safe, as well as the vault door, had two combination locks, and no staff member was allowed to know more than one on each.

In addition, it was mandatory that we change those numbers at least annually. Once the numbers were changed, they were written down, sealed in a special envelope, and sent by registered mail to the Regional office. This was, of course, in case something happened to the person who knew the combination numbers, so we wouldn't have a lockout.

This usually worked fine, but one day, one of our staff had to change the numbers on the vault door, and the next morning, we couldn't get the vault open.

I can't remember whether the person neglected to write the numbers down and had forgotten them, or perhaps had written the wrong numbers down. In any event, we experienced the dreaded "lockout."

The Farm Kid And The Flying Bank

As we locked up all of our files and cash before we went home every night, it was pretty much impossible to operate the branch. We finally had to contact the vault company, and they sent out a specialist right away, and he spent a whole day spinning the dial using various numbers until he finally got it about 7 that evening. I can't think of a more tedious job.

Anyway, thank goodness he figured it out because he told us that if he couldn't get it by later that evening, they would have no option but to go through the roof of the vault with a jackhammer. How nice that would have been, as our bedroom was directly above the vault.

The Bank was just across the street from two hotels, both with drinking establishments. Our evening's entertainment often consisted of sitting at the window and watching people leave the bar...particularly those in less than sober condition. It could be quite entertaining, to say the least.

We enjoyed Ponoka as we did virtually every place we lived. We became good friends with many of the staff as well as some of the farm customers. We were often invited out to a farm (or ranch) to go snowmobiling or just partying. Most all had small children, so Jean and Lory would usually go along with us.

Ponoka has hosted a Rodeo for many years...it being one of the larger ones on the rodeo circuit, running over 5 days around the beginning of July. Each year that I was there, I was asked to volunteer at the Rodeo Grounds—from taking tickets to working the beer gardens.

However, one summer the rodeo got pretty well completely rained out, and so many of us volunteers, along with many of the cowboys, ended up at one of the local drinking establishments.

We got to know several of the professional rodeo performers and lapped up the tales of their exploits as they followed the rodeo circuit around the World. Several of these pros were Americans, and I remember, in particular, one of the bull riders from somewhere in the far southern US by the name of "Myrtus Dightman."

As the beer flowed, the lifestyle sounded more and more exciting and, by the time I got home, much, much later and not in the best of condition, I had decided that I would leave the Bank and join the circuit. I wanted to be just like Myrtus.

Once Peggy got over her "mad", she thought my idea was exceedingly funny...especially when she found out that Myrtus was an African American.

It was while I was in Ponoka that we decided to get rid of the old Rambler American and get a bigger car. I believe we went to Wetaskiwin to car shop. We wound up buying a 1965 Pontiac 4-door Hardtop...quite a sporty car and a real step up from the Rambler.

12
BACK TO BRITISH COLUMBIA...

Well, you guessed it.....another personal letter from the Regional Office in 1969. This time, I was appointed Assistant Manager at Dawson Creek, B.C. Dawson Creek was a fair-sized branch, and the Manager was still Kurt Alfke... the same boss I had when I spent a few months there in 1962.

This position was pretty well a full-time lending job, starting with a relatively small lending limit above which I had to get Mr. Alfke's approval. Of course, he had a limit also, which I think was about $10,000....a pretty good limit for the time. Today, I expect that same branch would have a lending limit of well over $100,000, as I think that was my lending limit as a branch manager in 1989.

We rented a fairly decent house from a widowed lady who lived in Vancouver. We didn't see her often, but we never knew when she might show up. Not that it was a problem because we looked after the house pretty well, but it could be a bit annoying when we didn't know when she would show up. She also owned the house next door, which was rented by an RCMP fellow and his wife. Apparently, the landlady had a bedroom in their basement, and she would just walk in unannounced when she came to town—sometimes after they had gone to bed. That would be annoying.

I served as the Assistant Manager from 1969 until March, 1972 and, although I enjoyed the branch overall, I had some difficult days there. My predecessor had left Dawson Creek with a very good promotion.

Whether it was he or his predecessor, a trail of bad loans was left behind and I had the thankless job of trying to collect them. Nowadays the Bank simply hires repo specialists to seize vehicles or equipment to cover unpaid loans. However at that time the Banker had that miserable task and it wasn't a lot of fun.

The branch had a good client who ran the Ford Implement dealership and we would hire him and his truck to go with us to pick up machinery. A lot of money had been lent to beginner farmers in the Cherry Point and Silver Valley areas...just across the border in Alberta.

The loans were highly risky at the get go...like loans for very expensive tractors or machinery when the farmer had only a few acres under cultivation, and such other risky situations.

Very often the unpaid for equipment would be hidden in the bush on a neighboring farm and, on one occasion, we were met at the gate by a group of farmers who barred access to the farm. We could, if necessary, get the RCMP to accompany us but I don't recall having to resort to that.

We did have a few honest and trusted farmers in the area who knew what the bank was up against and would sometimes let us know if machinery had been hidden and where—which was a big help.

In one instance we headed out to seize a seed drill on a cold and miserable day in November. We found the drill OK but had a lot of difficulty winching it onto the truck and were freezing our butts off.

To add insult to injury, we could see the farmer watching us through his window and laughing at us.

After a few years my predecessor left the bank, but the damage had been done. The fact of the matter is that he was a really a nice fellow who had joined the bank about the same time I started in

The Farm Kid And The Flying Bank

Peace River and I knew him fairly well before I arrived in Dawson Creek. However, I had to question the lending skills of whoever granted these loans.

One day while the Manager was away on vacation I was approached by a customer who wanted a fairly good sized Farm loan to buy a bunch of sheep.

After reviewing his application closely I determined that his credit worthiness was questionable and I declined his application. Well, he waited for the Manager to return and got the loan from him.

During the following winter another of our clients came to the Bank and asked if we had financed this guy's sheep. I said that, yes, we had to which he suggested that we might want to check on them because he was aware that the borrower and his lady friend were spending a lot of time in a local bar and he hadn't noticed any activity at the farm for awhile.

So...out I go to have a look... Thank God it was March and everything was still frozen because all the sheep were starved and frozen to death.

Otherwise the stench would have been overwhelming.

We reported the situation to the RCMP and as far as I remember we simply wrote off the loan. I felt like telling my boss "I could have told you so" but I didn't.

Another time when the manager was on vacation I got a call one night that the branch in Pouce Coupe (about 5 miles away, and a sub-branch to Dawson Creek) was on fire.

I rushed to Pouce Coupe and by the time I got there the fire had been pretty well extinguished but the building was badly smoke damaged and unsecured and we had to get all the important files and whatever else we could get out to bring them back to Dawson Creek for storage.

As it was too difficult to move desks we were simply removing the drawers and piling them into a van but, every time we turned to getting the drawers from the desk of the Officer in Charge he would somehow divert us to other tasks saying he would look after his desk.

Well, when we thought we were pretty well done I realized that his desk had not yet been emptied so I yanked open a drawer to remove it and immediately realized that there was nothing in the drawer that needed saving - just a lot of empty beer and rye bottles.

The audit team arrived the next day and found a lot of other problems so he didn't last long with the bank and I had the task of temporarily running the branch once it was restored to a viable building. It was extremely frustrating to discover that scads of customers who had been declined at Dawson Creek had simply gone to Pouce Coupe and got the loans they wanted (even though almost all loans exceeded his lending authority). They were virtually all bad loans and, again, I had to chase down somebody else's dumb loans.

This guy was married and his wife was very strange (thank goodness they had no kids). The girls in the branch told me that when she was upset with her husband she would do things such as come down to the Bank and pull out all the flowers the girls had planted.

They were also the couple who kept their dog in the deep freeze until spring as it had died in the winter and the ground was too frozen to bury it.

During our stay in Dawson Creek I traded off the 1965 Pontiac for a 1969 green Ford which I drove until 1974. The dealership advertised the Pontiac on local TV with a photo of the car and promoted it as "Excellent condition, executive driven, etc. "They made is sound so good I almost felt like buying it back.

In the summer of 1969 Val and Keith came from Peace River and we went on a camping and fishing trip with them. I believe Mom and Dad looked after Jeannie & Lory again. We wound up at Francois Lake which was not far from Vanderhoof, B.C. We pitched our tent at Nithi Lodge, caught some fish, and overall had a good vacation.

We had a boy and girl, a perfect family we thought. However, on April 25th. 1970 our second daughter, Alison Jill, was born in the Dawson Creek Hospital. We both liked Jill for a name and the Alison was after a very nice neighbor girl at the Nampa farm.

She was a lot younger than I was but she was a pretty girl and very smart so Alison was a name that Peggy agreed to. We thought "Alison Jill McConnell" worked better than "Jill Alison McConnell."

However Jill has informed us many times that that was a mistake....she says she has to use Alison a lot because many businesses want first names. Heck, she was almost called "Nithi Lodge." She was several years younger than Jeannie and Lory and they have often hinted that she was spoiled. Perhaps she was...but she is very bright and a gifted artist and a great daughter.

That is not to say that they don't all have special qualities and we love them all equally.

Lynn Erickson, 17, (left) receives the annual trophy of a gold watch from assistant manager D. G. McConnell of the Canadian Imperial Bank of Commerce. Lynn is the aggregate winner of the South Peace 4H Club rally of June 27.

A photo from the Dawson Creek Newspaper, about 1970.

While I was in Dawson Creek I was introduced to the Kinsmen Club which in those days had an age limit of 40, and was affiliated with "The World Council of Young Men's' Clubs."

Peggy joined the Kinette Club there as well (Kinsmen wives) and our association with Kinsmen and Kinettes turned out to be a very enjoyable and rewarding experience. As we used to say, we worked hard and we played hard, and it was a great way to meet a lot of folks of our own age group.

The Farm Kid And The Flying Bank

The most rewarding part was lots of work projects within the community, and running fund raisers of all kinds in the community so we could carry on this work. All "fun" money for our parties, attending conventions and the like came from our pockets.... usually funds raised at our own Club functions.

Our affiliation with Kinsmen and Kinettes lasted for eleven years (until I got too old) and I will mention a bit more about that later on.

In about January of 1972 I received a phone call from the Regional Personnel Manager telling me that they would like to appoint me as the Manager of a new branch they were opening in St. Albert, Alberta the following March.

13

A BRANCH OF MY OWN

My replacement in Dawson Creek arrived about mid-February as the Bank wanted me to work with their Regional Office in hiring staff, ordering forms, organizing the branch, etc. This was a task I had not previously been involved in, and was a job I found quite enjoyable.

We started with a staff of about 7 people and had lots of applicants...almost all of whom were experienced CIBC staff who worked in Edmonton and lived in St. Albert. The official opening was held in March 1972, and the bank put on a great opening...ribbon cutting by the Mayor, coffee and goodies and the usual hoopla, and two "Chargex" girls from the Regional office dressed in their matching blue and gold uniforms acted as hostesses (Chargex later changed to VISA).

Bank Official opening day – March 20, 1972. Left to right: Ernie (Lynne's ex), Lynne, Dad, Mom, me and Peggy. Dig those dresses.

This photo was taken by the Bank's hired photographer the day of the official opening of the St. Albert branch. As this was a milestone in my career, I was well supported...From left to right: Dad, Mom, Uncle Alf Bird, Grandma Brown, Aunt Hilda Bird, my sister Lynne, her ex-husband Ernie, Peggy, me, and Grandpa Brown seated.

St. Albert is where we bought our first house...a 1200 Sq. Ft. Bungalow in Lacombe Park. I think the address was "60 Lambert Cres." It was brand new in a new development and lots of neighbors with young kids like us. St. Albert was, I think, the place we most enjoyed living in. It has grown by leaps and bounds since then but it had pretty much all we needed, and was only a short drive into Edmonton.

Mom and Dad were still living on the farm at Nampa in 1972 but by the following year they had left the farm and moved to Red Deer. We now were much closer to many of our relatives and that was great also. Peggy and I were again quite involved with Kinsmen and Kinettes which helped us get to know a lot of couples of our own age group fairly quickly.

Not long after moving into our new home the next-door neighbour and I decided to put up a fence around our lots, helping each other with the job. We rented a power auger for fence post holes and were making pretty good progress when we found out our telephones weren't working. Neither were those of many of our neighbors…That damned phone company again.

We called the telephone company and they sent out a repairman who quickly determined that we had cut through the telephone line and as it was our fault they could bill us for a healthy repair bill.

However, they were very considerate and didn't do so. The repairman did, however, point out that we had "skimmed" the main underground electricity line and came within a hair of electrocuting ourselves. Since that time, I have always called "Alberta 1 Call" before starting any such project.

Opening a new branch was very challenging in more ways than one. First and foremost, I was expected to "grow" the business, which meant visiting lots of local businessmen and farmers and hoping to land their accounts. The Bank of Montreal and the Bank of Nova Scotia had been in town for many years and were well established so it was a tough job.

There were a few farmers who dealt with CIBC in Edmonton and, once they were comfortable with me, moved their accounts to St. Albert. Also, being involved with the Kinsmen Club and getting to know lots of folks helped with getting new accounts.

The combination of a new branch with a relatively young and first-time manager was often a target for shysters who, I guess, thought we would be desperate for new business and would lend to anyone.

Fortunately, my lending experience as an Assistant Manager meant that I was pretty well prepared for this kind of thing, so when I was transferred out in 1974, I left a pretty clean loan portfolio.

In an attempt to attract new business, we stayed open until 8:00 PM on Fridays, so I seldom left the branch until then. Peggy and I developed the custom of getting a babysitter and going out for a Pizza (usually) and a bottle of wine as soon as I got home on Fridays. We were really "up-town" now.

It was during my tenure in St. Albert that we were instructed to give up our guns. We had to take all guns and ammunition to the local RCMP office, get a full receipt from them, which then had to be submitted to Head Office...I guess they needed to be sure none of us were keeping the guns.

In early 1974, I received a call from the Personnel Manager in Calgary who asked if I would consider a transfer to Inuvik, NWT. This at first sounded like a slap in the face, a demotion.

However, he suggested that the northern managers were having a meeting in Edmonton the following week, and their wives would be coming with them. He suggested that Peggy and I attend the social function associated with the meeting and Meet Brian and Gerry Rombough who we would be replacing and get the lowdown on Inuvik. I then had the choice of going or not.... the first time I was ever given a choice.

In any event, we discovered that Inuvik had about 15 on staff and the lifestyle was great and it sounded not only interesting but rather exciting. The Bank promised me that this appointment would be for a maximum of 18 months so we accepted their offer...and on to a great adventure for the whole family.

14
LIFE IN THE NORTHWEST TERRITORIES

I arrived in Inuvik alone around the end of January, 1974 and stayed in the Eskimo Inn...across from the branch. (Inuvik is Inuit for "Place of Man"). I spent a few days with my predecessor learning the ins and outs of banking in the north, and had to wait for his family to move out of the Bank house before I could bring Peggy and the kids up.

This occurred within a few days, and I then flew back to St. Albert to arrange for the sale of our house and the move to Inuvik. I was still driving the 1969 Ford car, which I left with a neighbor who said he would try to sell it for me. The Bank offered to move the car to Inuvik in the spring, by barge, up the Mackenzie River.

However, they were not prepared to have it flown up. There was no road to Inuvik in those days, although many years later the Dempster Highway was pushed through from Dawson City, Yukon. The only way in was by plane and goods were either flown in or shipped up the MacKenzie River by barge once the ice was gone.

At that time, you could not buy canned beer in Alberta but, because it was so much lighter to transport by air, that's all you could get during the winter in Inuvik. When the first barge came up the Mackenzie River in the spring, it was always loaded with bottled beer, much to the delight of the locals. I think it tasted the same, but not to the hardened beer drinker, I guess.

The Bank house in Inuvik was totally furnished, so we put most of our belongings in storage (at the Bank's expense, of course) and took only some clothes and a few personal things. The Bank also authorized me to buy a large grocery order, including a full beef, which they had flown to Inuvik for me. This was quite customary due to the high cost of meat and groceries in the north and the Bank house, in fact, had a large food storage room and two large deep freezes for this purpose. In addition, we were given a reasonable "northern allowance."

When we flew to Inuvik with our entire family of five, the Captain on the PWA (Pacific Western Airlines) flight was a fellow by the name of Bob Schultz, one of my fellow Kinsmen members in St. Albert.

When he found out we were aboard, he had the flight attendant bring each of us up, one at a time, to spend a little time on the flight deck with him and the co-pilot. Each of our kids was presented with a certificate from the airline certifying that they had crossed the Arctic Circle.

That made the trip kind of special. I was the last to go up and stayed there right through the landing in Inuvik. I am pretty sure that was against company policy, but it was a nice experience for me.

A few days after my arrival in Inuvik, I received a letter from Bob, the Manager who had taken my place in St. Albert. He enclosed a letter from the Regional Vice President addressed **to him**, congratulating him on achieving over $1. million in deposits, along with a note from Bob saying, "I think this should have been sent to you."

Sometimes it seemed like that's the way my career went.... work my butt off and somebody else gets the credit. A copy of the letter no doubt went into **HIS** personnel file.

It was quite interesting to experience 24 hours of daylight for a couple of months in the summer, and over 2 months of darkness in the winter. This didn't bother me a lot because even in Alberta, I usually went to work in the dark and came home in the dark in the wintertime.

Those long weeks of total darkness could be depressing for some folks, though. The 24 hours of sunlight in the summer was likely more difficult to adjust to....our kids would be playing outside with other kids, and then we would realize it was midnight with school tomorrow. Many people covered their bedroom windows with something to keep out the light.

I recall one weekend when I had gone to the office to catch up on work and was having lunch across the street at the Eskimo Inn with the Hotel owner. This would be around the end of February and, while we were eating, one of his staff ran in and said "Come look, the suns up!"

So...we both trotted over to look out the window to see a little sliver of red sun peaking over the horizon, and in 5 minutes or less, it was gone again. Of course, it stayed up a little longer each day until about June, when it never went down.

The Bank had one of the larger and better houses in Inuvik, and it was on Spruce Hill Drive, or what some called "Snob Hill." Our next-door neighbor, Jim Betteridge, was the local superintendent for Imperial Oil, and we became good friends with him and his wife, Marge.

The house was four or five blocks from the bank, and I always walked to work, which included taking the stairs up and over the "Utilidor." Because the ground was permanently frozen, underground water and sewer lines were not possible, so all utilities in town were run through the Utilidor—a metal-clad structure about 4 ft. by 4 ft., and on pilings about 4 feet off the ground.

One of the lines within the Utilidor was superheated water from the local generating station, which kept the fresh water and sewer lines from freezing. Many homes, including ours, were heated with hot water. The aforementioned super hot water line was run to our house and through a heat exchanger, which heated our own water supply. We had no furnace, per se.

The Farm Kid And The Flying Bank

The Utilidor

All buildings, including our home of course, were built on pilings that extended at least eight feet into the permafrost. If a heated building was not built on pilings off the ground, the heat from the building would melt the permafrost and it would sink into the ground. Consequently, no one had basements. Our house had a nice heated double garage with a ramp into the garage.

Besides the garage, the lower floor included the food storage area and a large family room with a TV. The upstairs was quite spacious, with three bedrooms and was the main living area. Oh yes...the TV. Well, it was in colour although we had but one station...CBC North.

A lot of the shows were "canned"—that is, reruns of shows that the people in the south had watched a week or more before. However, we did get Hockey Night in Canada live on Saturdays when we were there but even that was canned until not long before we arrived.

Inuvik did have a local radio station, with a lot of the programming being messages from one person to another, as there were no phone connections between the settlements in the north at that time.

Some messages were quite interesting and sometimes entertaining. Things like: "to Silas in Inuvik, I have returned from the trap line with 17 fox. Please bring a couple of skinning knives when you fly to Tuk tomorrow"...and things like that. ("Tuk" was the short form for "Tuktoyaktuk").

Almost everyone who lived in or visited Inuvik or Tuktoyaktuk went home with a sweatshirt that was emblazoned with "TUK U" and smaller lettering that said "Tuk University."

Of course, it was only a gimmick as there was no such thing as a University. But we were happy with the schools, and when we were transferred out of Inuvik, Jean and Lory were a bit ahead of the kids in the Alberta school.

However, the Hospital—that was a bit of a different story. The Doctors were hired by the

Government and we often thought that if they were any good, they would be far better off running their own clinic.

One day I was working at the office on a weekend when I suddenly had a terrible pain in my lower abdomen. I tried walking home and was almost there when my neighbor, Jim Betteridge, offered me a ride. Normally, I would have declined, but I was thankful that day.

Consequently, I wound up in the hospital and it was subsequently determined that I had a kidney stone. One of the tests that was performed involved injecting me with some kind of iodine-based dye that they could track on X-ray. The Doctor, a female French-Canadian, was doing the injecting with a syringe that I'm sure held a full cup of dye.

The X-ray technician suggested that the needle end be taped to my arm but she was rebuffed by the doctor. As she started pumping the dye in the needle backed out of my vein and into my muscle and I experienced the most excruciating pain imaginable. The needle was taped down for the next attempt.

Jim visited me two or three times a day and kept reminding me that they (Imperial Oil) had a plane at the ready if I wanted to be flown out to Edmonton.

However, within a couple of days I was fine so that wasn't necessary.

Sometime in May before we were transferred out Jill developed several lumps on her neck (she would have just turned five). A Dr. deStefano attended her and said he would have to lance them, and an appointment was scheduled.

However, a couple of days later, the hospital experienced a nurse's strike so the surgery was postponed. Shortly thereafter, we were transferred out and we took Jill to a Doctor in Edmonton. It turned out that it was an infection of some kind, and an antibiotic prescription did the trick. A few months later, we read in either the Edmonton or Calgary paper that a Dr. deStefano had been deported to Italy for practicing in Inuvik without a license.

As an aside...there was a nurses' residence in Inuvik and, like every other business up there, there was always a large turnover of girls...all single to the best of my knowledge. Anyway, the residence was known as "The riding academy." Just sayin'.

The Farm Kid And The Flying Bank

Our house in Inuvik

When we were there, Inuvik had a navy base consisting of some 250 enlisted men, and many of them had their families with them. Why it was called a navy base, I have no idea, because they certainly did not have any ships. Their actual "base" was a few miles out of town in a very restricted area. Government houses were provided for the married men, and single men lived in an apartment-type complex. The Officer's mess was off limits to those below the rank of Captain (I think) but, as there were only 6 officers, they opened it up to a maximum of 25 local businessmen as "associate members."

I applied to join and was put on a waiting list. However, as Inuvik was a very transient town, it didn't take more than a few days to be accepted. It was a great facility, and a great place for meeting the most important businessmen as well as the senior officers of the base.

Around 4 PM every Friday, the Bank of Montreal Manager would come along and say, "C'mon...it's TGIF time." At the mess we would buy cocktails for .35¢, and usually play poker (could not lose more than $10.), and the kitchen detail would bring in food...usually chicken, hamburgers, and the like.

Every Saturday, there would be a first-run movie, and once a month, a candlelight dinner where the gals wore their long dresses and we dressed in our best formal wear, to sit down to a 5 or 6-course meal including wine.

Once a month, the Base would bill the Bank for my expenses and the bill, considered my monthly PR expense, would be paid by the bank.

The base also brought in some top-notch entertainment for the folks in the service, but such shows were always open to the public, free of charge. During the 16 months we were there, Canada's acrobatic aerial team, the Snowbirds, were there twice.

The Farm Kid And The Flying Bank

We were especially honored in the summer of 1974 when the Bank's Chairman and his wife came to Inuvik in the Bank's jet. We had them for a nice dinner and arranged a tour of the town for them. We subsequently received very nice personal letters from the Chairman and his wife.

A copy of the Chairman's letter is appended below. Accompanying them on this trip was the Regional Vice President from Calgary, Frank Duncanson and his wife.

Something that we found amusing—they wanted to go to a bar and stay until after midnight so they could walk out into the sunlight.

Dennis, Frank Duncanson (Regional Vice President for Alberta & North West Territories), Peggy, and Bob Dixon (a junior employee) in front of the Bank's jet.

HEAD OFFICE · COMMERCE COURT
TORONTO, CANADA
M5L 1A2

J. PAGE R. WADSWORTH
CHAIRMAN

July 17, 1974

Mr D. G. McConnell
Manager
Canadian Imperial Bank of Commerce
Inuvik
Northwest Territories

Dear Dennis:

When we returned to Toronto after our most interesting trip to the Territories we took off for a couple of weeks holidays at our cottage, hence the delay in writing to you. I did want to thank you for all the arrangements you made for our visit to Inuvik, and in particular for the presentation made to us at your branch which will remind us for many years of the warm welcome we received. Perhaps the enclosed picture may be of some interest.

It is most gratifying to see the Bank's prominent position in Inuvik and I know this is due in no small part to the continuing job being done by you and your staff.

The trip to Resolute was of particular interest and we were able to cap off the Yellowknife visit with a half day's fishing in Great Slave Lake. Again, many thanks.

Yours sincerely

The Farm Kid And The Flying Bank

Lory and Jill in Inuvik. Note Jill's "Mother Hubbard" parka.

Contrary to some people's belief, the summers in Inuvik, while short, could be very pleasant. It was not unusual to see temperatures in the 70's F (20 / 25 C) and even up to 80 F (25 + C) on occasion. The town had three or four kid's ball teams, and both Jean and Lory played on "the Utilidors" team. On one occasion, I was asked to be the umpire behind the plate, which I reluctantly agreed to.

Well, I was not a very good ump and took so much verbal abuse from the parents that I never volunteered for that job again. Lory also played hockey while we were there and continued to play both ball and hockey after we moved to High River. However, he just was not an aggressive player and so he soon elected to drop out of both. The ironic thing is that when Megan, his first child was born, he said, "And I'm going to get her into sports just like my dad did for me." In fact, Megan did play T-ball, but I think that was about it.

Another thing that surprises a lot of folks about Inuvik is that it is considered to be in a Desert area. Precipitation there is quite low, and, in fact, the first winter we spent there, I never had to shovel the driveway. The snow didn't amount to much more than hoar frost in the air that settled on the ground. We did have more snow the second winter but likely much less than there was back in Alberta.

One afternoon in late winter a helicopter pilot for a local company dropped in to the Bank to see me. He wanted to know if Peggy and I would like to go to Tuktoyaktuk with him the following Sunday to take in their Winter Festival. He also had room for one of our kids so, as Jean and Lory had already been on trips with the Flying Bank, we took Jill with us. She was almost 5 at the time. We had never been in a helicopter before, but jumped at the opportunity.

However, we became a little uneasy when he couldn't start the motor and used a piece of haywire to hold something together so it would start. But...no worries - it was a great flight on a sunny day, and he took us on the "scenic" route...pointing out such things as pingos and Oil base camps. We landed on the ice right next to where everything was happening. Snowmobile races, dog sled races, the high kick contest, and even a fox skinning contest. A very enjoyable and memorable day, and we were home by dark.

From Wikipedia: A pingo, also called a hydrolaccolith, is a mound of earth-covered ice found in the Arctic and subarctic that can reach up to 70 metres (230 ft) in height and up to 600 m (2,000 ft) in diameter. The term originated as the Inuvialuktun word for a small hill. A pingo is a periglacial landform, which is defined as a nonglacial landform or process linked to colder climates.

Periglacial suggests an environment located on the margin of past glaciers. However, freeze and thaw cycles influence landscapes outside areas of past glaciation. Therefore, periglacial environments are anywhere freezing and thawing modify the landscape in a significant manner.[1] They are essentially formed by ground ice which develops during the winter months as temperatures fall.[2][3][4] The plural form is "pingos."

Pingos are generally hollow, and there is a good-sized pingo in the village of Tuktoyaktuk. Some years previous to our first visit there, it was thought it would make a good" indoor" year-round curling rink. However, the hoar frost constantly dropping from the ceiling made the ice pretty much unplayable, so that was a bust.

When we were there for the first time, we were taken on a tour inside, where many caribou carcasses and fish were stored, and it served, in fact, as a year-round freezer for the village.

The Farm Kid And The Flying Bank

One of the Bank employees inside the Pingo in Tuktoyaktuk

Because of the remoteness of this posting, we didn't have many visitors from home. I always regretted the fact that Mom and Dad never made it up for a visit. However, we did have a couple of visitors. Uncle Cliff worked up there for awhile as a cook for an oil company and we were very happy to have him drop in on us.

That same winter a school chum from Nampa, Alan Gardner, who, I think, was running a cat for somebody up there for awhile also dropped in one day. While we were up there we experienced the first Christmas ever that we weren't together with Mom and Dad and other family members. However, most of the bank staff were in the same boat so that winter they were all family. We had the biggest house so many of them had Christmas dinner with us. We also used to have several of them over to watch Hockey or Football on CBC.

Inuvik was a magnet for lots of foreigners and business folks from various countries because of it's uniqueness…particularly the matter of the Utilidor system, which other countries with land north of the Arctic Circle wanted to emulate. And I expect that many folks came just because the Government (theirs or ours) paid their way. One time, we went to a Chamber of Commerce dinner at which some 15 or 20 Ambassadors from as many countries were present.

Peggy sat beside the Governor of the Bank of Iran, and I beside the ambassador from Nigeria. A very nice man but his halitosis was something else.

While we were in Inuvik, a rather funny incident occurred. Several women in the community complained of getting obscene phone calls (Peggy never got hers), and they thought they recognized the voice, but nobody seemed able to put a handle on it.

Well, when the culprit was finally caught, he turned out to be one of the local CBC radio announcers. Kinda dumb, I would say.

The Farm Kid And The Flying Bank

I had a typist in the bank by the name of Kay
Wilson and we became good friends with her and
her husband, Bob. One day in July of 1974, I was
talking to Bob (who worked for Finning Tractor)
and he mentioned that he would love to go on a
fishing trip before he got transferred out.

I am not much of a fisherman but one day Mike
Zubko (the owner of Aklavik Air) was in my office
and I asked him what it would cost to take us on a
fishing trip. His comment, as I remember it, was
"by golly, I haven't been out yet this summer
myself. How about Friday night after work, and it
won't cost you a thing."

That day just happened to be Lory's 9th.
birthday, and Mike said there would be room for
him as well. Of course, we had 24 hours of sunlight
at that time of year, so we took off after supper and
flew northwest for almost an hour, which, at times,
was a bit scary as Mike flew low over several little
lakes with the plane on its side as he looked for fish.

He finally found a promising little lake, and we
landed there—on Floats of course. The lake was full
of Lake Trout, and it didn't take long for all four of
us to catch all we wanted. Mike was adamant that
we clean all the fish right there...leaving the entrails
for the seagulls, and making sure we left no garbage

of any kind behind. We have some great old movies of Lory cleaning fish on Mike's instructions, with a look of disgust on his face as he pulled out the guts. All in all, it was a great trip and one to remember. We were home before midnight.

Lory and his fish - somewhere Northeast of Inuvik, NWT. July 15, 1974

The Farm Kid And The Flying Bank

I had left my 1969 Ford with a friend in St. Albert to try to sell for me wanting to get at least $1,200. Well, it never sold which turned out to be a good thing, as we then had transportation when we came down for vacation.

In about August or September of 1974, after our vacation, I took the bank up on their offer to transport the car to Inuvik by barge. It was trucked to Hay River, and then put on a barge and up the Mackenzie River to Inuvik. About the only thing the car was used for was to go grocery shopping. I had a nice, large heated garage so I kept the car nicely shined up.

In fact, one day I drove it to the local Liquor store, and when I came out of the store, there were four or five teenagers admiring the car, apparently thinking it was brand new.

In fact, it was by then about 5 years old, while many of the local taxis were much newer. However, there was no pavement, and all the taxis were driven with reckless abandon and seldom, if ever, washed, so my car stood out.

In the spring of 1975, I knew I would be transferred out soon, so I listed the car for sale. The ad attracted a young lady who wanted it for a taxi, and she offered and paid me $1,500. no questions asked.

We assumed we still had a few months to go before we were transferred out, so I knew a local bush pilot who was leaving Inuvik, and he had an older Mazda he needed to get rid of. I think I paid about $700. for it and sold it for about the same price when we finally moved.

One evening, we picked up Wayne and Wendy Paulsen (Wendy was the branch accountant, having replaced Brian Butchart, who was there when I arrived). I think we were going to the pub...can't really remember where we would be going. In any event, we ran into a little problem when the fan belt broke. Almost without hesitation, Wendy whipped off her pantyhose, Wayne rigged them up as a fan belt, and away we went. I think it was replaced before we sold the car.

My customer from Tuktoyaktuk, Eddie Gruben, was in one spring day and invited me to go whale hunting with him. I was a bit leery as I knew that they were usually hunted in nothing more than a canoe or kayak.

However, Eddie assured me that he had a larger boat with a cabin on it, so, yes, this sounded like an interesting thing to do. He would contact me as soon as the whales came in (These were Beluga whales). Anyway, I got transferred out before the whales "came in" …I was not sure if I was disappointed or relieved.

The town of Inuvik circa 1975. We lived on the horseshoe-shaped street about middle of the photo. The line you see behind buildings on our street (and others) is the Utilidor. The Mackenzie River is in the background and a small lake behind our house.

15
BANKING IN THE NORTH

The Bank was established in Inuvik in the early sixties, shortly after the town was established. In those days, a manager was appointed on the understanding that he would remain single, and would stay for a minimum of two years, during which time they did not get out for vacations, etc., but, instead, would get a couple of months' vacation when their term was over.

As it turned out, most of these men decided to stay in the north, some even marrying local girls, and, when transferred back to "civilization," they would resign from the Bank and go back to Inuvik to work for somebody else. So, in the early 1970's, the Bank changed its approach. They built a very nice house adequate for accommodating a family of at least 5 or 6, provided the same vacation time as bankers in the south, and paid for the entire family to fly to Edmonton or Calgary and back up to twice a year. I believe I was the third "family" man to be appointed manager in Inuvik, following Brian Rombough and Gerry Pears before him.

During the 16 months we spent there, my family had 3 trips out at the bank's expense, and I had eight altogether for managers' meetings, and the like.

Banking in the north truly was different. We often lent money to the natives, but more often than not had to be patient to get it back. The population in Inuvik at that time was about 4,000, of which we were told about 1/3 were white, 1/3 Inuit, and 1/3 Dene Nation Indigenous people. To many of these folks, time did not mean a thing.

It was not uncommon to have loans on the books that had had no action for two or three years and were almost impossible to collect when the borrower was out on the land somewhere.

However, the borrower might show up out of the blue one day and pay off the loan, and then expect to borrow again. Individual client files were well maintained, so we usually knew if they could be depended upon to show up to pay "eventually." When interest was not paid for 3 consecutive months, the account had to go on a special report, and this would drive the credit Department in Calgary nuts.

I have often seen borrowers show up after two or three years to pay off an old loan. We sometimes lent extra money that was kept in an account to cover interest until the loan was eventually paid off. Somewhat unorthodox, but it kept the credit department off our backs.

In one similar instance, we had a loan on the books for about $300. that had long since been written off. One day early in the New Year, the borrower showed up and wanted to borrow another $200. I was incredulous until he showed me his T4 slip for a job he had had with an oil company, and where they had deducted about $600 for taxes. Knowing that he did not have to pay taxes, I went to the Post Office and picked up an income tax form. I filled it out and had him sign it, showing his address as "in care of the Bank".

I lent him the $200. and when the quarterly "bad loan" report went in showing an increase, it prompted an immediate phone call asking if I had lost my mind. I can't remember what my exact response was, but within a month or two, the Tax rebate had arrived. The loan was paid off, and the customer had a few bucks left over, and all was well. I think I may have even received a phone call from a different guy in the Credit Department complimenting me on collecting a bad loan. As I said, banking is different in the North.

Because the population in Inuvik was quite transient, with folks transferred in and out with various companies...sometimes for only a month or two at a time, there were not a lot of privately owned vehicles in town. Consequently, there were about 40 taxis...a lot for some 4000 residents. Virtually all company vehicles were pickup trucks. A lot of folks would walk to the grocery store, and then call a cab to get their groceries home. The majority of the cab drivers were European, many from Yugoslavia. They often fought over fares, and sometimes you were caught in the middle of a very heated argument when all you did was hail a cab. One of those drivers was a guy by the name of Rudy Rapo.

One day, Rudy came to see me as he wanted me to finance a used gravel truck he was buying. I spoke to my neighbor, Jim Betteridge, that evening and he confirmed that, yes, they were hiring Rudy and his gravel truck to work on an Oil site. So I lent Rudy the money ($3,500.) and took an "assignment of accounts receivable" which would enable the

Bank to collect from his employer if he didn't pay. Rudy signed reluctantly but asked that I not register it with Imperial Oil, as they may not hire him. Notwithstanding my better judgement, I agreed to this.

One evening at home, a couple of months later, Jim dropped over and asked if Rudy had paid me off. He had not. Whereupon Jim advised me that Rudy was on his way to Edmonton to collect his cheque and return to Yugoslavia.

However, he said that he was heading to Edmonton right away on the Company plane, and he would take the Assignment form to their office before Rudy got there. This worked great...except that Rudy now did not have the money to leave the country. He came back to Inuvik, directly to the Bank, and threatened to kill me. One of the girls in the office saw what was happening and called the cops and two of them showed up and hauled him away. His parting words were *"You will never forget the name of Rudy Rapo"*...and you see, I haven't.

Our customer, Aklavik Air, who supplied the light aircraft for our Flying Bank (discussed in the following Chapter) also owned a Twin Otter aircraft, a very hardworking Bush Plane built for the

North. One of our tellers was the spouse of Aklavik Air's usual Twin Otter pilot who one day dropped in to ask if I wanted to go with him on a run up the coast on the weekend. I had the privilege of riding along as one of only three passengers, with the rest of the craft loaded with fuel and supplies for various coastal oil camps and government scientific sites. The co-pilot seat was occupied by a senior man from one of the oil companies and was planning to spend a few days at one of the camps. I occupied that seat on the way home.

The other passenger who sat directly across from me was a girl of about 19 from Quebec. We struck up a bit of a conversation and she let me know that she was going to be the cook at one of the government scientific sites on the Arctic coast. So…I asked her if she had had training as a cook or Chef, to which she snapped back, "No. I have 14 brothers and sisters, so I fucking well know how to cook! "OK - No more questions."

I didn't expect to be making any "Farm Improvement Loans" in Inuvik but, in fact, I did. The loan was to a "Silas Kanaganas" who was a Reindeer herder. He had two or three other Inuit men working with him and they followed a Reindeer herd around and, when it was time to slaughter some of them, he would radio in to a Government Office and somebody would fly out to the herd (usually in a Twin Otter), slaughter the animals, and bring the meat back for sale. Most of it was sold in northern stores but after we left Inuvik, we actually saw reindeer meat in a Hudson's Bay store in Edmonton and the package clearly said "Producer – Silas Kanaganas."

The loan was to purchase a herd, a practice set up by the territorial government to create businesses and jobs for the native folks. Silas and his crew would come off "the land" about two or three times a year to pick up supplies (I believe they would radio in for a plane on skis to pick them up) and they were interesting fellows. Other than these infrequent trips to Inuvik, they lived off the land and their dress was old traditional Inuit. All handmade caribou hide parkas and mukluks. Not unlike the following photo.

The Farm Kid And The Flying Bank

16
THE FLYING BANK

Unquestionably, my posting to Inuvik was the most interesting, the most exciting, and the most memorable. This was due to several factors, one of which was the fact that we operated a "Flying Bank." Apart from a few months in the dead of winter when there was no daylight, we hired a small plane every month from our customer "Aklavik Air" to take us to Tuktoyaktuk, Fort McPherson, and Aklavik.

Two of us would go to work, setting up in the local library or a school for an hour or two before we flew on to the next stop. We usually had room for a couple of extra passengers so our spouses and my kids all had the occasional chance to fly along with us...usually spending time surveying the village or visiting a local craft store until it was time to leave. Depending on the time of year, we flew in planes with wheels, skis, and floats.

As there was no telephone service to these communities, we would mail out little flyers to post in the local Hudson's Bay or Co-op store ahead of time. A day or so before our planned trip, we would put a message over the radio outlining our expected arrival times in each village and asking "someone" to meet us at the plane.

During the time I was there, there was only one time when nobody responded. We had no sight seeing passengers that day, but I and the gal that went that day had no choice but to start walking towards the village of Fort McPherson. The pilot said he had another trip to make and would be back in 2 or 3 hours. It was a muddy road and the cash box was heavy (we always brought along a lot of coins for the stores) so there we were, trudging along through the tundra carrying the cash box between us.

Fortunately, someone came along with a pickup truck after we had walked a mile or more, and they turned around and gave us a lift.

A couple of years before I reported to Inuvik the Bank had initiated the Flying Bank Service, after success with one in Yellowknife earlier. The Yellowknife Flying Bank actually operated out of a scheduled Northern airline whereas our Flying Bank utilized the services of a local air service, "Aklavik Air", owned by Mr. Mike Zubko, a customer of ours. We let him know a bit ahead of time (after checking weather and Flying conditions for the chosen day), and Mike would arrange to make sure one of his several planes would be available for us. We did not fly during mid winter due to lack of daylight but would start up each spring around mid March.

The "Flying Bank" was really a losing proposition, but was set up mainly to appease the territorial government. We did little more than supply coins to the stores and cash the odd cheque.

We did have a very good customer in Tuktoyaktuk by the name of "Eddie Gruben." He was an Inuit and a very astute businessman. He owned at least two or three gravel trucks and, because he was inuit he was usually the first one hired by oil companies. He also owned the school bus in Tuktoyaktuk. He would meet us at the airstrip in the bus and one of his first questions was usually "Who do you need to collect money from today?"

He seemed to always know who had just got paid from whatever source so I would tell him who was behind in payments and he would drive us to the borrower's residence, sometimes getting him out of bed after a payday binge, and haul him into the bus to pay me. Yes, I think I *said* banking in the north was different.

One time we took the flying bank to Sachs Harbour on Banks Island, a settlement of about 143 souls. (all Inuit except for a government appointed settlement manager and a couple of men running the MOT airstrip). We had a few very good customers at Sachs Harbour as well, as they often made very good money trapping fox.

The most prosperous of them was a fellow by the name of "David Nasagalowak" who usually had over $100,000. on deposit with us, which was a princely sum in those days. Every few years, he would buy a new pickup truck and there were only two miles of navigable road from the settlement to the MOT airstrip. Snowmobiles were also plentiful...when something went wrong with one, they would simply buy another.

It is said that often, both here and elsewhere, the "old" machines were left on the ice only to fall to the bottom of the ocean, lake, or river when it thawed. Peggy and Lana Butchart (the Accountant's wife), along with the Branch trainee, went on that trip with me. The trainee was left to cash the odd cheque while I visited around the settlement.

Our trip that day was on a Cessna 337, commonly called a "push-pull" as it had two props, one in front and one behind the cabin. Our pilot thought he would provide us with easier access to the village, so instead of landing at the MOT airstrip, he decided to land on the ocean ice next to the village.

It turned out that no one had used the ice strip for some time, and it was covered with about three feet of snow.

Well, he got us down safely, with snow flying in every direction, but why we didn't crash I will never know. Other pilots later told us that it was virtual suicide to try to land a wheeled plane in snow that deep.

Then the problem was getting it back in the air when it was time to go home. A number of the Inuit folks came down with their snowmobiles, shovels, and sheets of plywood. After lots of shovelling and laying down the plywood, the pilot, sans his passengers and the heavy cash box, finally managed to lift off and land at the MOT airstrip, where we were taken on snowmobiles and sleds to meet up with the plane for the trip home. While trying to extricate the plane from the snow, several of us grabbed the bar between the tails to push and bounce it to help it get going. Peggy said, *"Now I know why they call it a push-pull."*

When the pilot gunned the motor, it blew me right over top of an Inuit lady on a snowmobile. Fortunately, neither of us was hurt.

We later learned that that particular pilot was fired by Aklavik Air for another similar "death-defying" stunt. He then went to work in Whitehorse, where he subsequently cracked up in the mountains and killed himself. I must say, the other pilots we used were much more trustworthy.

Plane stuck at Sachs Harbour – me in the forefront

Peggy and Lana Butchart with the fox pelts they bought at Sachs Harbour from David Nasagalowak Polar bear hide behind them, which we could have bought for $400

Every 20 or 30 years (maybe more), the Bank (CIBC) hires an author to update the Bank's history. In 2017, that person was Mr. Rod McPherson, who reached out to me when he learned that I had worked in Inuvik. Here is the story I gave him (condensed and edited) that made it into the History Book.

Jack McIntosh, personnel manager at the Regional Office in Calgary, phoned Dennis McConnell in 1974 to ask the manager of the branch in St. Albert, Alberta, if he would take a transfer to Inuvik. McConnell's first reaction was: "What have I done wrong?" McIntosh invited McConnell and his wife, Peggy, to a meeting of northern managers in Edmonton the following week. There, the McConnells met the current Inuvik manager, Brian Rombough, and his wife, Gerry. After talking to

The Farm Kid And The Flying Bank

the Romboughs, the McConnells agreed to move to the Northwest Territories with their three children.

As manager of the Inuvik branch with 15 employees, McConnell was immediately a community leader in the town of 4,000. "You were one of the head honchoes. You were invited to Chamber of Commerce dinners. We met ambassadors from all around the world," he said. He was also a member, along with local business leaders and officers from the Canadian Forces Base, of the officers' mess. On Friday nights, there were candlelight dinners, entertainment, and cocktails that cost only thirty-five cents.

One Saturday each month, McConnell and an employee operated a flying bank. They'd spend all day travelling to Tuktoyaktuk, Fort McPherson, and Aklavik with ninety-minute stops at each. Banking was conducted in the local library, co-op, school staff room, or Hudson's Bay store. On occasion, the flying bank went further afield to Sachs Harbour on Banks Island.

The small planes hired from Aklavik Air were equipped with wheels, skis, or floats, depending on the time of year. Landings by the pilot on ice airstrips could be rough, or the plane might get stuck in snow or mud. One time, when McConnell was helping move a mired Cessna 337, he got bowled over by the prop wash from the rear push-pull engine.

McConnell travelled with a fifty-pound metal cash box containing $300 in coins and $3,000 in bills for *loans and cheque cashing. Sometimes they'd have to lug the box on foot into town from the airstrip if no one came to meet them. Loans and collections could be unusual. One farm improvement loan covered a reindeer herd raised for meat. In Tuktoyaktuk, an Inuit client, Eddie Gruben, had such local clout that he helped McConnell with an overdue loan. Gruben knew a particular debtor had just been paid the day before, took McConnell to the debtor's house, roused him from his bed, and said: "Pay Dennis." He did.*

McConnell retired in 1997 after serving in Alberta and British Columbia as branch manager, inspector, and area manager, but those sixteen months in Inuvik were the most memorable of his thirty-eight-year career with the Bank.

17
BACK TO ALBERTA

In late May of 1975, the transfer letter arrived. The Bank had kept its promise...I would be serving only 16 months in Inuvik before I was to report to the High River, Alberta branch as Branch Manager. This was a well-established branch that had been there for many years and most of the clientele were farmers or in businesses related to the Farming Industry.

Apart from Inuvik, most of my postings were in agriculture-dominated areas, and that is the Industry that I came to know best and felt the most comfortable with. We had a staff of about 12, but the lending portfolio was much larger than at previous branches. High River was also becoming a commuter town for folks working in Calgary, so our mortgage and personal loan portfolio was growing quite rapidly.

It wasn't long before the Regional Office agreed to transfer in a person to look after the consumer portfolio, and that's when I met Gerry Carmichael, a good addition to the branch who went on to become a fairly senior officer with CIBC before retiring several years after I did.

When I first moved to High River, I was expected to join a local service club and, as there was no Kinsmen Club there, I joined the Lions. Shortly after doing so, I heard that several fellows who had been Kinsmen elsewhere decided to start up a new club, so I soon resigned from the Lions and became a charter member of the new club.

Of course, we were looking for new members, and I had just met a young fellow (10 years my junior) who had just moved to town and was banking with us.

So... I sponsored Larry Kowatch as a new member, and he and his wife Bonnie have been close friends ever since. Larry was in the Oil business and retired fairly early. They also go to Arizona in the winter and spend their summers near Rocky Mountain House, where they were both raised. We have gone on many holidays with them...firstly taking our kids to Disneyland in 1979, and later on going on many golfing holidays with them. We spent a lot of time with them over the years, most recently on a trip to Newfoundland.

The Farm Kid And The Flying Bank

As mentioned in Chapter 13, the Kinsmen Club was affiliated with many other Clubs throughout the world via the "World Council of Young Men's Clubs." I was the club President for the 1976/77 fiscal year, and I believe it was about the end of January 1977 when our club received a letter from Kinsmen Headquarters advising that the Round Table Club of Britain and Ireland (RTBI) was celebrating its 50th. Jubilee (anniversary) and were inviting about a 100 World Council couples to be hosted for a full two weeks from late May to early June to help them celebrate. They invited five couples from Canada, and our National Executive would choose those couples from all applicants based on their commitment to Kinsmen, etc.

The letter was presented to the club, but as virtually all of us had young children in school, there were no takers. Peggy was working at the High River hospital and one day mentioned this to her friend Kay Hamilton, with whom she worked. Kay urged us to apply, assuring us that she would be happy to stay at our place and look after our kids if we were able to go.

By this time, Jean was about 14 and was already a big help around the house, so Kay was confident that she could manage. She and her husband were childless, so that made it easier for her.

To make a long story short, we happened to be one of the five Canadian couples selected to go. All we needed to do was to pay for our flight to London and back. We decided we would take as much vacation as we could and see as much of Europe as we could.

I was entitled to four weeks, but requested another week's leave of absence from the bank. Because I was so involved with a community service club, the bank actually granted me that extra week as a fully paid vacation and even gave me a couple of hundred dollars to subsidize our costs.

There were three separate bus tours and we applied for the England/Scotland tour but missed out on that and ended up on the England/Wales tour. We were billeted at Round Table members' homes...a different area and different hosts every night for two solid weeks.

We did, of course, get to know people from around the world who were on the same "coach" and, to the best of my memory, some of the countries represented on our coach were India, Zambia, Germany, Luxembourg, Sweden, US,

Australia, Surinam, and one other Canadian couple from Labrador City - what a great experience and our hosts refused to let us pay for anything. We couldn't keep up with them in the beer drinking department, though. We spent a week in London upon our arrival, then two weeks on the continent, then back to England for our Round Table experience.

The trip ended with a huge Luncheon at the Guild Hall in London, the same venue where the Queen hosted her Jubilee Luncheon that year...complete with trumpeters in the balconies and lots of pomp and grandeur.

What a trip!

Without going into a lot of detail, we were able to do many more things for the community. Although I thoroughly enjoyed my eleven years in Kinsmen, I wasn't overly upset when I turned 40 and had to resign. The Kinsmen Club in later years removed the age limit and severed its ties with the World Council.

During those years, the Canadian songbird, Anne Murray, was doing TV commercials for the Bank, and we were thrilled when we were advised that she would be coming to High River to shoot one of her commercials. She arrived with several film crew members and a fancy motor home served as her quarters. With approval from the town, a section of the main street in front of the bank was closed to traffic, and shooting began.

Needless to say, it drew quite a crowd, and I believe they had to make several takes before they got one without some idiot bystander shouting out something dumb in the middle of one. I also remember they had to take an unwelcome break when the train came through town...and it didn't just go through town, it spent some time shunting cars back and forth.

When the "shooting" was over, one of the crew handed me a hundred dollars and told me that it was Anne's birthday as well as her anniversary, and asked me to pick up as many bottles of the best Champagne that would cover.

As soon as the branch closed for the day, the crew produced a birthday cake, I had picked up the champagne, and we had a party for her in the branch. We found her to be a wonderfully friendly person, and we won't soon forget that day.

Anne Murray and the High River Staff

Anne & some of her "crew" in the branch.

18

TO THE BANK'S INSPECTION DEPARTMENT

Sometime in 1979, another personal letter arrived from the Regional Human Resources Department. I was appointed "Assistant Inspector" in the Regional Office Credit Department in Calgary.

This appointment did not, for the first time, require a change in homes. It was about a 30-minute commute to Calgary, but one of the Inspectors who I would be working with in Calgary was Bruce Anderson, who also lived in High River. So Bruce and I carpooled to work, driving to South Calgary and taking a transit bus downtown to where our office was on the 3rd or 4th. floor in the old CIBC Main Branch Building at 309 – 8th. Ave. S.W. Later during this posting, we took the new "C-train" instead of the bus.

This job entailed reviewing and approving credit applications coming in from a group of branches within the Region, up to, as best as I can recall, $200,000. There were about 5 Assistant Inspectors, each responsible for some 25 or so branches. Each branch manager, depending on his pay grade level, size of the branch, etc., had his or her own specific lending limit above which the applications were sent in to us.

As I was new to the job, all credit applications that I worked with were reviewed by an Inspector to ensure I had a handle on what I was doing. For the most part, this Inspector turned out to be Bruce, who, within a very few days, gave me his vote of confidence, and I was on my own. Each Assistant Inspector had a Credit Assistant who first looked at the incoming applications to ensure the proper financial information and the like were included before the file landed in my "inbox."

Above me were Senior Assistant Inspectors, Inspectors, Senior Inspectors, and a Credit Superintendent...each with successively higher approval limits. In addition to making the final approval on loans up to $200,000, I did the preliminary review of credit applications up to $400,000. before they were handed up the line. In essence, every Credit application was looked at by at least two officers before the approval (or decline), along with special conditions and the like, was returned to the branch.

I don't think I was in the job for more than about 6 months before I was promoted to "Senior Assistant Inspector," and within a year or so, I was again promoted to "Inspector."

I didn't mind working in the Regional Office as there was a general feeling of camaraderie, and a change from running a branch was good for awhile. But there were some uncomfortable times too...the one that I remember most vividly was when I became leery of the lending habits of one of the managers in a branch that I was responsible for. I reported my concerns to the Superintendent, who had me visit the branch and check things out myself.

Unfortunately, the manager was a fellow whom I had worked under for a few months in the branch system and he was a great guy, really. However, he let a couple of accounts run substantial unauthorized overdrafts, which were not at all well-based and later resulted in some pretty big losses to the Bank.

As a result of my visit, he was demoted immediately....in fact, he likely would have been fired but as he was close to retirement, the Bank simply assigned him to a somewhat menial job in the Regional Office until he reached retirement age. That was a particularly uncomfortable situation for me, but the branch was my responsibility, so it was his head or mine.

19
THE LETHBRIDGE CHALLENGE

Sometime in 1981, I was summoned to the Senior Vice President's office. Mr. Nordheimer advised me that they would like me to report to the Lethbridge, Alberta main branch as a "Deputy Manager". This was a promotion even though I would work under the branch Manager, (name withheld). This manager had a reputation for being a bit of a tyrant to work for.

However, he welcomed me by acknowledging that he looked forward to my good background in lending, as I would be responsible for a very large lending portfolio, which included Farm and Business loans for all three of the Lethbridge branches, and I would have three assistant managers reporting to me.

He was the manager of all three branches and had a fairly high lending limit, which, for all intents and purposes, was entrusted to me. In addition to supervising the assistant managers, I had a credit officer reporting to me who did some of the preliminary work on my accounts. This was a position in which I directly handled several very large corporate accounts and involved some big-dollar lending. The largest account I had was for a Regional Airline (later taken over by CP Air, I believe), which included a 20-million-dollar loan to buy an aircraft. I think I handled the job well and, in fact, received some very favourable performance reports from the Manager.

But things change. By the time I had been at the branch for two or three years, it was pretty obvious that the manager and one of the female staff members had more than a "business" relationship.

I ignored the situation, but one day I received a call from the then Senior Vice President (John Lowrey) advising me that he had received an anonymous letter filling him on this situation. He wanted to know if I could comment on it, and I could only say that "yes, I could see why someone would have written such a letter." This resulted in the manager being called in to the Regional Office and his subsequent return to the office was not pleasant.

He was determined to find out who had ratted on him and he developed a Nazi-like interrogation program where, one by one, each staff member was taken to a basement room and interrogated at length. For some reason, he was sure that I was the culprit and life at the branch then became miserable, to say the least. He *was* a tyrant.

Fortunately for me, Mr. Lowrey was aware that until this time, I was receiving good performance reports and he phoned me at home more than once to see how things were going. He knew that life was getting unbearable and asked me to hang on for a couple of months, by which time he had a good posting in mind for me.

20
LIFE AS AN "AREA MANAGER"

True to his word, by the fall of 1985, the bank had reorganized and would now operate with "Area Managers," and I was appointed as one of six in Alberta, with total authority over the operations at 31 rural branches, from Ponoka in the north to Milk River in the south, and from border to border east to west.

My area of responsibility did not include city branches, so Lethbridge came under another Area manager, which was just as well. The new job meant a lot of travel, which I enjoyed for awhile, giving me the opportunity to see a lot of the Southern half of Alberta and meeting a lot of staff members in the branches.

However, after about twice around my area, I grew a bit tired of staying in some less-than-top-grade motels and eating in a lot of greasy spoons. The worst experience in this respect was when it was about 40 below and I had to leave the motel and get into an ice-cold vehicle, and bump along on squared tires to find someplace to have breakfast. But the job had its perks as well.

Working out of the Regional Office I was sometimes given tickets to NHL games in Calgary, albeit only because the senior folks above me couldn't use them. I was also included in customer-related golf tournaments at Kananaskis, and the like.

In fact, the highlight of this posting was that I was in Calgary during the 1988 Winter Olympics. That year the bank sponsored the ladies Alpine ski team and, as an area manager, I was included as a "dignitary" at a special luncheon with these athletes and other Olympic-related functions. The bank also bused several of us to a couple of Alpine events, at their expense, to "wave the flag" for CIBC. We were all given CIBC logoed toques and scarves.

It was during my stint as an Area Manager that I had my first run-in with Computers. Personal computers were beginning to become popular, and we knew that the Bank was getting more and more into the computer age, so one day, Al Hathaway, one of the other Area Managers, and I decided we needed to educate ourselves on computers. We went together to a computer store, of which there were not many in those days, and wound up buying identical computers. I believe they were known as "286" and a far cry from today's models.

It was a slow and arduous process, and there were many days I could have chucked the damned thing out the window.

One day, Al got hold of a pirated copy of "Leisure Suit Larry" - a rather risqué game for the times but we had lots of fun with that for awhile. By today's standards, it was pretty elementary—no sound and you had to type all the commands. There was no such thing as "Windows" but, rather, a DOS system was used. But I stuck with it and eventually got interested in spreadsheets, in particular, and who would have thought that 9 or 10 years later I would have my own computer-based business.

I still have a small desk ornament that Mom gave me in those early computer days that says "LORD, GIVE ME THE STRENGTH TO GET ALONG WITH COMPUTERS."

By 1989, the Bank had decided to reorganize again…this time eliminating the Area Manager idea but establishing "District Managers" who had larger areas and more authority.

My immediate boss by then was Linda Hohol, A Senior Vice President. She discussed my next move with me…suggesting that they would like to transfer me to Grand Prairie to act as Manager of the Branch and District Manager for the Peace River country.

This would have been a pretty good promotion for me, but Peggy did not want to move that far away from our kids and grandkids, and I was convinced that she was right.

Rather, I knew that the manager in Ponoka was on sick leave, and I asked for the opportunity to take his place. For the first time ever, I had the opportunity to decide where I would go next.

Although Ponoka was one of the branches I was responsible for as Area Manager, it was actually in the same pay grade, so it was a lateral move, which I thought I would stay with until retirement.

At that time, it was the largest agricultural CIBC branch in Canada with several multimillion-dollar feedlot accounts, most of which would be administered by one of three assistant managers who reported to me. I dealt directly with only a handful of the larger accounts.

The Farm Kid And The Flying Bank

In about 1990 we started going to St. George, Utah, for our vacations, as they had great golf courses there and have since added several more. About 45 minutes away through the Virgin River gorge is Mesquite, Nevada, where there are several more great golf courses and several casinos.

We would go with Val and Keith, or our friends Larry & Bonnie, and play golf several times a week. It was also a great place to do some wonderful hiking and not far from places like Zion National Park, Bryce Canyon, and the like. St. George was growing rapidly, and the six of us decided it would be a good idea to buy some property there.

We had a few hoops to jump through...like getting US Social Security cards in order to buy property, but that only meant going to the US consulate in Calgary and lining up with a bunch of immigrants ...but the process was relatively easy. I still have my card, which is clearly stamped "not for working purposes." We made an offer on a nice condo, but it was sold before our offer could be presented. But we trusted the realtor, who then faxed me details of places he thought we might like—there was no email in those days.

The six of us agreed, sight unseen, to buy a condo and were able to do all the paperwork by fax and mail. He even located a renter for the place, as none of us were ready to retire yet.

That fall we went down with Larry and Bonnie and when we checked on the place, we found it was in a condo development with lots of young families and lots of little kids running around, not exactly what we had in mind, so we put it back on the market and it didn't take long to sell.

We each pocketed a bit of capital gain within a year, so that worked out OK. Val & Keith later bought a park model in St. George but as they didn't usually go down until February, we were able to use it a few times.

21
BACK TO BRANCH MANAGEMENT

Not long before my arrival at Ponoka, I, as Area Manager, had the distasteful task of initiating the dismissal of one of the former Assistant Managers. His manager had given him very favourable reports due to the significant increase in his loan portfolio and the substantial loan fees he managed to collect, essentially far exceeding his targets for the year. Consequently, he was promoted to a Branch Manager position at a branch in southern Alberta.

However, at a branch visit shortly afterwards, I was asked by the credit department to have a look at the portfolio as they had some concerns.

It didn't take long to find some major problems…very large loans to undeserving individuals who were happy to pay a substantial loan fee—most of whom had no intention of repaying the loans and, in fact, much of the recorded information was fictionalized in order to get the loans through.

Loans were insufficiently secured, and most were subsequently partially or fully written off. We suspected that the assistant manager may have been getting kickbacks for his shoddy lending but this could not be proven.

However, he was immediately dismissed. Truth be known, I think this may have led to the Manager's breakdown and long-term sick leave and he was never able to return to work.

I had a pretty good team of Assistant Managers, one of whom had been at the branch for several years. What I saw as our primary responsibility was to see what could be done about recovering as much of these loans as possible, and we went to work with some good lawyers and were pretty successful in finding ways to collect a good deal of these losses.

In fact we recovered almost two million dollars, which was thought lost and on more than one occasion, I was complimented by officers in the Credit department…one even suggesting that this success was a big feather in my hat and should be reflected in my performance reports and annual salary review.

Well, unfortunately, the Credit Department did not do my annual review.

I was visited one day in 1993 by the District Manager and, totally out of the blue, he let me know that the Vice President had decided that I wasn't buying into some changes to the way the Bank operated...primarily changes to do with the treatment of consumer customers...borrowers and depositors. This basically amounted to rating our customers as to value to the Bank (i.e. Class A, B, or C) where the level of service and fees charged, etc., would depend on their "Class."

Admittedly, I did not fully agree with this (an idea which I am fairly sure has long since been abandoned) but, because we were behind some branches in fully implementing the change it was an excuse to route me out. I was essentially told that this was more important than the two million dollars in bad loan recoveries.

I knew this was a ploy to get me out of the way for the manager of a smaller branch who had a University degree and was, admittedly, deserving of a good promotion.

However, because he had not been with the Bank for very many years, he was earning much less than I so it would be a money saver for the Bank.

I told the District Manager as much and was told that that was not the case but rather, the job would go up for bids. I was offered two years' salary to get lost. That would have been great but I was only 52, so I could not draw a pension until I was 65. That meant working at who knows what for another 13 years.

The bank's Pension plan left a lot to be desired...one could get a full pension at age 61 if applied for and approved (which was pretty well automatic as they were trying to dump most of the older people), or could get a reduced pension as early as age 55. If one left the bank before age 55, then they could not draw a pension until they turned 65.

Needless to say, this all came as a terrible gut-wrenching shock. This was a very humbling experience for someone who had virtually dedicated his life to the Bank for over 35 years. I was able to negotiate an alternative, which was to demote me and cut my wages so I could work until I was at least 55, when I could draw a pension, albeit somewhat reduced from a full pension. That's how I ended up as an Assistant Manager in Rocky Mountain House for three plus years.

To add insult to injury, so to speak, when I announced my plans to retire, the bank tried to persuade me to stay as they had trouble finding a replacement. I did stay until I was close to 56, but I was sick of the Bank and left with a bitter taste in my mouth.

Many of my peers had received a tidy buyout package a year or two earlier when they reached age 55—full pension PLUS two years' salary. I lobbied for the same treatment but was told that the funds for that buyout program were used up and besides, they wanted me to stay.

How could I not be a bitter retiree? Oh yes…guess who got the job in Ponoka? I guess I should be thankful that at least my pension was based on the highest five earning years.

I guess there is a silver lining in every cloud. I was thankful that I was no longer in Ponoka when the BSE thing hit the beef industry hard. Several of those multimillion-dollar accounts in Ponoka went bankrupt and I'm sure it was a nightmare for my replacement.

22
BECOMING AN ENTREPRENEUR

I retired not knowing what I would do, but I was confident I could survive. Bill Carrington, the golf pro at the local Pine Hills course, was a customer of ours at the bank in Rocky Mountain House and one day before I retired I mentioned to him that if he needed someone at the Golf course I wouldn't mind a summer job. I was thinking that they might need a course marshal but he called one day and asked if I wanted to work in the pro shop.

The pay wasn't very good, but I knew that going in and I had my bank pension to fall back on. It wasn't a bad job, and it included all the free golf, with power cart, I wanted.

However, after standing on the concrete floor of the pro shop for some pretty long days, I was often too tired to take advantage of it. Anyway, as the golf season wore down he laid me off, which I knew would be the case.

One day, about the time I left the golf course I received a call from Stan Gasior who had retired from CIBC in Sylvan Lake a few years earlier due to health reasons. Not long after he retired, with his health problems behind him, he had worked for a year or two for the "Alberta Hail and Crop" office in Lacombe on some farm lending program they had initiated.

That office had just called him to see if he wanted to come back to work, as they needed additional help with a new program which was the "Farm Income Disaster Program" or FIDP. He was not interested, so he called me and suggested that I might want to look into it. I made a call and was invited in for an interview the next day.

I was essentially hired "on the spot" as it was a good fit for me with my past experience dealing with the agricultural industry, and I was comfortable with using a computer. I was a "Claims Verifier," and after about two days of training, I was pretty much on my own.

As was the case with my stint in the Bank's Credit Department, I had an approval limit above which I had to refer the file to my supervisor.

I spent only five months during the winter of 1997/98 working at that job, during which time I was given progressively higher approval limits. I continued to live in Rocky Mountain House and commuted the one-hour trip to Lacombe every workday. Fortunately, the winter was relatively mild, and I never ran into bad roads all winter.

While on the job, I soon realized that many farmers were getting poor service in having their claims paid – mostly because they did not understand the program or the multitude of forms that had to be completed and in most cases, neither did their accountant.

I later learned that most accountants simply gave the job to a back-room office girl and very few of them fully understood the program. Consequently, it sometimes took months for a claim to be paid, usually with a myriad of phone calls between the FIDP office and the farmer.

Furthermore, it was very often the case that farmers were shortchanged in the payment to them simply because of missing information which they could not or would not provide.

Often, when it looked like I could legitimately increase a claim with more information, a call to the farmer would be met with a suspicious attitude...I'm sure most of them thought I was looking for ways to *reduce* the claim.

Around the end of March 1998, I resigned from the Government job and sent out some advertising offering my services in assisting with the claim application. I developed a computer program on my own, into which I built checks and balances to make sure the information provided made sense (e.g., the amount of feed used had to be appropriate for the number of cattle owned and the length of time they were fed, and that kind of thing).

The claim could not be prepared until the farm had its income tax return completed for the previous year (the claim year), and the program deadline was usually September 1st. so that is the period I had to work within.

That first year, I knew there had been an agricultural disaster in the Peace Country, as an extremely wet spring in 1997 had kept many farmers from getting their crops in. I sent 8,500 unaddressed flyers to every rural address in the Peace Country and sat back and waited for the responses. Out of those 8,500 flyers, I received a grand total of 30 inquiries.

This was disappointing, but I decided that would be enough to pay my expenses so I lined up several farmers to meet with during a 10 or 15-day period and Peggy and I left for the Peace Country.

I usually managed to do two claims a day (occasionally three). I would gather the information needed and get the application signed and then spend the evenings in the motel room preparing them for submission.

Invariably, the claim amounts calculated exceeded the customers' expectations, which eased the pain of meeting my fees. Those first claims were virtually all paid within a week or ten days and that was my best advertising.

As soon as I got home, the phone wouldn't stop ringing. That began seven hectic yet rewarding seasons, during which I often earned far more in a few months than I had in a year at the bank.

The job involved making lots of photocopies of previous year's tax returns, grain and cattle receipts, and the like. This kept Peggy busy while I was crunching numbers, and we worked pretty well as a partnership...well, that is apart from the times that I relied on her to navigate with county maps. But I won't dwell on that. That first year, we didn't make a lot of money because I was afraid to charge too much. But I learned quickly, so the next 5 years were pretty lucrative.

At the end of the first year, I received a call from my former boss at the FIDP office who wanted to know if I was finished with preparing claims for the year and, if so, would I come back to work for them. Needless to say, I would not be allowed to review any claims that I had submitted. I accepted her offer and went back to work for them until almost Christmas time.

I would have stayed there another month or two, but I knew that the hog industry was in trouble and would have lots of claims, so I received permission from my boss to send out some advertising...on the firm understanding that I would not look at any claims until I had resigned from FIDP. The first response to my advertising was a phone call, which Peggy answered.

She told the caller that I was at work, and when he asked where I worked, she told him. As luck would have it, the caller was the Provincial Minister of Agriculture... whoops. The next day, I was called into the boss's office, and *her* boss was there.

Although I had received the OK to send out the advertising from *my* boss, the big guys decided that was a conflict of interest, so I was asked to resign by the end of that week. The first time I'd ever been fired.

However, my relationship with the FIDP office remained cordial and was a big help in getting complicated claims (such as multi-faceted corporate farms and the like) sorted out.

In the seventh year, the disaster program underwent major changes, and a lot of my clients were unsure if they wanted to get involved or not, so my business dropped off a bit. As this work was pretty much seasonal, it allowed us to get away in the winter and in the spring of 2005, on the drive home from Arizona, I decided that I had had enough...especially if the business was going to slow down.

When I got home, I called a gal whom I had worked with in the FIDP office in Lacombe to see if she was interested in buying my business. She had called me the year before to see if she could work for me, but I didn't feel that I needed the help. Anyway, my call was timely because she was preparing to resign and go into competition with me, and we readily agreed on a price.

By this time, I had a portfolio of 450 clients...not bad for an "idea" I had 7 years previous. I heard recently that she is still in business and apparently doing just fine.

Rocky Mountain House was fairly central for our business, as we had clients from High Level in the North to Milk River in the south. However, once we sold the business, Peggy wanted to move closer to Calgary, where our three kids and all of our grandkids were living.

I had played golf at Carstairs a few years previously and knew it was a nice course and easy to walk. We were also looking for a condo that would make it easier for us to get away in the winter without worrying about who we could get to shovel snow and check on the house regularly. Carstairs fit the bill in all three of those circumstances, so we sold our home in Rocky and moved here in July 2005.

23
THE SNOWBIRD YEARS

During my later years in the bank, I had several customers who were retired or semi-retired who spent their winters in the southern US...mainly California and Arizona. I wanted nothing better than to get away from snow and ice and bad roads, so I was determined well before I retired that I, too, would become a snowbird. I also loved to golf, so I could continue to golf all winter. Some customers played ball all winter as well, and that appealed to me also, but the parks I stayed in initially did not have ball teams, so I just never got into that.

One day in 2000, on one of our trips home from the Peace River country, we were going through Valleyview, and we noticed a nice 1996 "Fifth Wheel" trailer with a "for sale" sign on it. We stopped to look it over, called the owner and struck a deal.

However, I had nothing to pull it with, but he said he would deliver it to Rocky Mountain House, where we still lived at the time. It was a 36-footer with three slide-outs and quite a comfortable unit.

Now we had to look for a truck and, within a day or two had bought a 2000 model Chevrolet one-ton crew cab with dual wheels that we had seen advertised by a dealership in Wetaskiwin. I had a fifth wheel hitch installed and we were ready to "hit the road."

Our unit parked on a friend's acreage at Rocky Mountain House, and the rig at a Duncan family Reunion at Blueridge with our "California room" attached.

While I was ready to head south that same fall, I was a bit apprehensive about heading out with this big rig into unknown territory, and I kept finding excuses that kept us from getting away. If only I had somebody who knew the ropes that I could travel with.

Well...we endured one more winter, but used the rig a few times during the following summer. In fact, our first trip was to meet Jill and Andy (her ex) at Dickson Dam, where they were camping for the weekend with some friends. All went pretty well until it was time to set up camp. It took a while to get the fridge going and figure out how to run everything, but I managed to do fine. That is...until I decided to hook up the sewer.

I undid the cap on the sewer outlet and out gushed about three gallons of old sewage.... what a disgusting stinky mess...I managed to avoid getting it all over me, but I sure gave my hands a good soapy scrub. But there we were with a disgusting little puddle of crap that stunk to high heaven. There were some folks tenting close to our unit, but fortunately, they were away from their campsite at the time. Peggy had brought along a box of powdered bleach...what a godsend.... I believe I used the whole box, but it did quell the stench. I pity whoever camped in that spot next.

By the time the winter of 2001/02 rolled around, I had built up some confidence, and we were truly ready to become snowbirds. Peggy's cousin and his wife, Harmon & Lou Duncan, had been going south for many years and were heading for Yuma, AZ, right after Christmas. They suggested that they would be happy to travel with us and had a friend in Yuma who would find camping spots for us both. For some reason, can't remember why, we headed out a day earlier than the Duncans with plans to meet in Yuma.

It also happened that neighbors of ours in Rocky Mountain House had a park model in a fairly nice little RV park at Quartzite, AZ, and they wanted us to stop there for a few days. I had checked the weather and road conditions for Alberta and the states we would travel through, and rechecked several times. The weather was sunny and was supposed to stay that way, and the AMA website showed all roads clear and dry.

So away we went and got as far as Great Falls, Montana, the first day. We found a food store with a large parking lot and got permission to park there for the night. We got away quite early the next morning and were making good time until we reached Monida Pass on the Montana/Idaho border.

We noticed icicles hanging from the signs and realized that we were getting into freezing rain...and the road got treacherous. The first little knoll we crept over there was a truck and 5th. Wheel, not unlike ours, lying on its side on one side of the road, and an overturned jeep was on the other side, a short distance further on. I had managed to stop before we hit the worst of it and put the truck into four-wheel drive, geared down, and white-knuckled it. Fortunately, the bad roads ended within a few miles, and we sailed on again.

We dragged the fifth wheel south for three years (2002, 2003, and 2004), never leaving before Christmas and staying a bit longer each time. The first year, we spent only January and February in Yuma as noted above. The following summer, we heard of some other folks from Rocky Mountain House, both avid golfers, who were spending their winters in Twenty-Nine Palms, California. It's not the greatest place in the world, but there was a decent campground, and if you stayed there, you could play the adjoining golf course as often as you liked for $179. a month.

Peggy had pretty much quit golfing by then, but I golfed almost every day for the approximately two and a half months we were there. We came back to Twenty-Nine Palms the following year, and that time stayed for about three months.

Our friends, Al & Lynda Anderson, had a home in Mesa Shadows Mobile Home Park in Mesa, AZ, and, in a roundabout way, questioned the sanity of spending the money and aggravation in hauling this big outfit all the way to Arizona or California and back home again.

It was somewhat costly at about 7 miles per gallon, but as snowbirds, we thought that was the thing to do. And at that time, our Canadian dollar was only worth about 65¢ US.

After a number of incidents with the rig, we finally decided to take their advice. Incidents to be sure, let me tell you about them:

I've already mentioned our initial camping experience with the sewer episode.

I've also mentioned the freezing rain we encountered on our first trip.

Still on our first trip, we came to a point on the highway with a sign that pointed straight ahead and said "Needles,"…a town in California that was on our route.

Well, it was straight ahead, so I gunned the motor to climb the rise in the highway, only to realize at the last second that we were going over the highway and had to turn left at the top of the rise to go towards Needles. Here was a T intersection, and I was going far too fast to make the turn. Fortunately, there was enough room to go straight across onto a rough and semi-gravelled area that gave me enough time to bring the unit to a halt. No harm done, just a helluva scare.

We arrived safely in Quartzite, found the RV Park our Rocky neighbors were in, and found a parking spot, albeit in an overflow area. We enjoyed the couple of days there, even taking in a local music jam. When we were ready to pull out, I tried to raise the landing jacks with the electric system so I could hitch up. All I got was a clicking noise, so I assumed the gears were stripped. No problem.

I had a couple of hydraulic jacks with me, so I got it pretty much jacked up when Larry, our Rocky neighbor, thought he knew what the problem was, so he ran to his park model to get some tools. While he was gone, I decided I would use the toilet in the trailer, so I was standing there in the bathroom doing what I went there for when all of a sudden there was a helluva bang as the trailer slid off the jacks.

We had forgotten to block the wheels. Again, no real damage was done other than to disturb my call of nature. Anyway, Larry's idea did not solve the problem, so we blocked the wheels, jacked the unit up, hooked up and headed for Yuma.

We arrived in Yuma in jig time and found Harmon and Lou and got parked and hooked up where we were to stay for 2 months.

Shortly after our arrival, Harmon asked if I used electricity for the water heater, pointing out that electricity was included in our rent, so there was no sense using propane. We found that the electric heating element was burnt out, so we went uptown and got one for a few dollars. To install it, we had to remove the propane burner, which was easy to do.

We got the element installed and checked it to make sure it worked. Then we had to reinstall the propane burner, after which I went into the trailer, flicked the switch to turn on the propane to make sure that it still worked. We heard it start up, so, so satisfied with a job well done, we sat down in our attached California room to enjoy a beer. We hardly had a chance to enjoy our cool one when a fellow from a neighboring parking area came on the run to tell us the trailer was on fire.

We knew immediately what had to have caused the fire, so I instinctively ran in and shut off the propane while Harmon ran outside and unscrewed the water inlet hose from the trailer and got the fire out. We then discovered that the orifice had fallen out of the burner when we took it off and when I turned the water heater on it created a blow torch-like flame climbing the side of the trailer.

The damage was fairly severe but the fire did not have a chance to burn through the outside wall so we were able to pick up filler and paint and managed to fix it reasonably well ourselves. We subsequently made it home without further incident.

The following year, we headed south from Rocky Mountain House the day after Christmas. We wanted to make as many miles as possible that first day so we left about 5 AM on a -25F day. Before we left, I had noticed that the clip holding one of the landing jacks up was pretty worn, but I decided I would buy a replacement part when I got to warmer climes.

So it would have been about 5:45 in the morning, still very dark, when we crossed the Garrington Bridge between James River Bridge and Bowden. We hit a bit of a bump as we went over the bridge, and when I looked in the rear-view mirror, we had a glorious shower of sparks shooting out about 100 feet behind us. The damned landing jack had fallen down, and by the time I got stopped the foot piece was pretty well worn right through. Unfortunately, the landing leg had bent, and despite the efforts of a couple of passersby, it was impossible to straighten it or push it back in place, and we couldn't go on with the leg dragging on the ground.

Finally, a highway worker came along and tried to help...again to no avail, but by this time it was about 7:30 so I could get a hold of Woody's RV in Red Deer on my cell phone. They confirmed that they had a replacement part but that I would have to have a welder cut off the bent leg before I could move.

As luck would have it, the highway worker was standing at my window and overheard the conversation, and by the time I had finished on the phone, he had hailed a welding truck and the welder had the leg cut off and was rolling up his hoses. He would not take anything for his efforts but after leaving about $500. at Woody's, we made it as far as Claresholm, Alberta that night.

Each time we hauled the fifth wheel down, we planned to spend a night or two at St. George, as we knew the area, and it would be warm enough to de-winterize the trailer. The valve to shut off the sewage discharge was getting very hard to open, so I had bought a new one while we were at Woody's in Red Deer and, again, thought that St. George would be a good place to change it.

While we had an RV lot with water and sewer, I got permission to make the change on the concrete at their dumping station. I got a rug out of the trailer to lie on as I gingerly took the discharge piping apart to remove and replace the old valve. Sewage was dripping out, but as long as it didn't land on me, I didn't worry about it.

I finally got out the last bolt and pried the line apart, and with a disgusting "whoosh," I was drenched in sewage. This time it was our own, but it didn't smell any better. I had no choice but to finish the job...gagging a bit as I did so. The rug and my clothes were done for, but how could I go into the trailer this way?

Peggy came out with a change of clothes, I disrobed and hid from the public's view as best I could as she hosed me down and I changed into dry clothes. The old ones went in the dumpster, and after a good shower and another change of clothes, I was good for travel.

By the third year, we had grown somewhat smarter and, of course, experienced but on the way down, we ran into about three or four hundred miles of terrible road conditions through Montana, Idaho, and part of Utah.

We drove slowly in a lower gear and four-wheel drive, and that was no picnic – especially when it came to downhill grades in the mountains. We made it through without incident apart from aching arms and frayed nerves but that would be our last trip to Arizona with the rig.

The following summer, we hauled the RV to a Brown side family reunion west of Edmonton and, when we went to leave, we ran into the same problem as we had at Quartzite. Lory was there to help us as we jacked up the trailer to hitch it up.

We decided to block the front as it was raised...he on one side and Peggy and I on the other. Dummies that we are, we again forgot to block the wheels, and all of a sudden the whole unit (it only weighed 14,000 pounds) began to slide off the jacks towards Peggy and me and landed with a bang. Lory was sure we had been crushed, but fortunately, we managed to get out of the way in time.

Now we blocked the wheels and tried again, and managed to get hooked up and hightailed it for home. Just before we sold the unit, we discovered a crank in one of the holds that was there for a reason...the unit could be cranked up manually if the electric motor didn't work. Too soon old and too late smart.

I once envied the folks who had those fancy RV units, but I no longer do. We managed to sell the truck and trailer in 2005, and that was the end of that.

Harmon and Lou usually spent a month in Mesa after they left Yuma with their fifth wheel and always stayed in "Fiesta RV Park" where several of Lou's relatives wintered. It was on University Drive and just east of Val Vista. It is now part of Val Vista Village.

The Farm Kid And The Flying Bank

In the spring of 2004, before we headed home with the RV, we stopped at Fiesta and bought an old park model for $1,000. The unit belonged to relatives of Lou's who had bought a newer model and had been trying to sell it for $2,000.

It was pretty rough and needed some TLC, but it had a heat pump, which provided adequate heat and cooling so we drove our van down in the fall of 2004 and spent the winter there while we looked around for something better. Our plan was to sell the old park model if we could and buy a newer park model with an Arizona room in that same park.

During the summer at home in Alberta, I listed the old Park Model in the Calgary Herald for $6,500. and must have had close to 100 inquiries. It sold sight unseen to a single fellow. Now we had no place to stay the following winter, so we contacted Al & Lynda to see if they knew of anyplace to rent for a month or two until we could find something.

They contacted Marion and Maggie Jamison from Iowa, who didn't come down until after Christmas, and, although they did not normally rent their place out, they agreed to rent to us for a month. That gave us time to look around and by mid-December had bought a single wide Mobile Home (Unit #118) in Mesa Shadows on 4th. Street.

We flew home for Christmas and took possession when we returned on January 1st. 2006.

So after spending three winters in our RV, we were now Arizona homeowners, so to speak—(the pad was rented). We did a fair amount of upgrading to the unit, but in March of 2010, we decided to move into a double wide Mobile Home, so we bought a nice unit (#233) in the same park, and that was our winter home until we decided to sell and give up on snow-birding in the spring of 2016.

Our unit #118 was purchased by Don and Lois Bratt of Calgary, and our Unit #233 was sold to an American couple.

I can say that we did have many good winters in Mesa Shadows, spending a lot of time with our long-time friends, Al & Lynda Anderson and met a lot of other nice couples. I did a lot of golfing, we had many 'happy hours" and lots of card playing. We were entertained at various shows at the centre in our Park as well as at several other parks. As our park was one of the smaller ones we didn't draw the "big names" as did some other parks but we did have Brenda Lee and a number of other great entertainers.

The Farm Kid And The Flying Bank

I think it was the winter of 2011 or 2012 that Al, having been in the radio and TV business, came up with the idea that we should have a talent show in the park. So we put up a poster inviting anybody interested to sign up for an act of their choice. Some chose Karaoke, some put together very good skits or musical presentations, etc. We had no shortage of participants, and the event always quickly sold out. (We only had to give one act the hook- we were suspicious from the start when he arrived on stage with a life-sized blow-up doll).

Al and I became hosts of a very successful show for several years. We always had a skit or act of some kind of our own. Some pretty good ones, and some not as good—the latter were Al's ideas, I'm sure. Actually, Al was usually the idea man. When we were planning our first show, he called me one day to let me know that he had a good idea for a skit we could do. He went on to say, "One of us has a speaking part, and the other is a dummy— guess which one you are."

The first year we rented formal wear, including patent leather shoes and the works. We subsequently hosted as "the Booze Brothers", "the Smothered Brothers", the Elderly Brothers and the final year as Dennis & Al.

24
SETTLING DOWN IN ALBERTA

We moved to Carstairs, Alberta, in 2005 and have no plans to move anytime soon. At this writing (March 2026), I am 84, and Peggy is 80.

So here we are, happily ensconced in Carstairs. Jean moved here shortly after we did, and she works out of her home for an Investment firm headquartered in Ontario. She does a lot of travel by both air and car. Jeannie never married but is a full-time career woman and is happy living on her own.

Lory was married to Diane Ling and they had three children, Megan, Nicole, and Robert. Lory and Diane had been separated for many years and divorced some years before Diane passed away in 2015 at the age of 50. Lory is now married to Mindy (Malon) and they live on an acreage just north of Cochrane.

Lory has been involved in the stucco business for many years and, more recently, expanded into all types of exterior work. About 2 years ago, he turned the business over to Robert. They still work together and are doing very well. Both are hard workers with a good reputation in the industry and thus have lots of work. Mindy owns her own Hair Salon in Cochrane (Mindy's Place) and is a great homemaker.

Jill married Andy Dunbar in 1993, and they had one child, Connor, who is now 32 and a few years ago transitioned to "Claire." Jill and Andy moved to Fort McMurray several years ago and have since divorced. She subsequently married Sean Carbery, and they have one son, Chase, about 15. Sean was born and raised in that country and has a good job with SunCor.

About 2½ years ago, they bought an acreage property at Skelton Lake, much closer to Edmonton and not so far for us to travel. For now, it is a "retreat" while they spend most week-ends providing needed TLC and it will become their residence when they retire in a few years.

Dad's Story From The Nampa History Book - Pages 899 And 900

"I arrived in Peace River, March 9, 1928, with my father, Jack McConnell, my uncle Tom Hall and cousin Charlie Hall. We brought two carloads of settlers' effects with us, including 12 horses, a cow, two sows and a crate of chickens.

It was a long, slow trip from our prairie home at Davidson, Saskatchewan. The railway let one person travel free with each car; however, we all had to get there, so you can figure out for yourself how my cousin Charlie and I arrived. Things went slowly, but smoothly, until we arrived at Smith, AB. There, they stopped for dinner. Would you believe that out of the 20 settlers' cars on the train, 35 people came to the restaurant to eat!

After that, the train crew asked a lot of questions, but that was all. When the train pulled into Peace River, the front end stopped on the bridge, and my uncle said, "Time to get off, boys!" We jumped, but didn't realize there was a fifty-foot grade at that point, so we rolled down the bank through the rose bushes, brush, and gravel. Not a glorious entrance, but the price was right.

We didn't know what to expect, as none of us had been this far north before. We finally got the cars spotted at the loading platform, which was down under the bridge in the area then known as Moccasin Flats. After unloading the livestock, we went exploring the town, had supper in Ma Nagle's cafe, and parted with two dollars of our last remaining ten. We set up a tent, and that was our home for the next two weeks.

We had a variety of jobs in the following weeks and finally got a contract building the elevator sidings at Roma and Grimshaw.

My mother, brothers and sisters arrived in late August of 1928. We continued in the contracting business until the spring of 1931. Times were very tough, and any job that was available had so many after it that you practically had to work for nothing. In April 1931, we rented the Pop Trowsdale farm, the south half of 4-82-20, and that was the beginning of our long association with Nampa.

Our family consisted of my brother Alex, who now lives near Victoria, B.C., my brother Clifford, who still calls Nampa home, although he has retired from farming; my five sisters, Pearl, who married Redford Hawath and lived at Olds until her death in 1932; Mary, who married Jim Owen and now lives in Lacombe; Gladys married George Talbot, and they now reside in High Prairie. Grace married Fred Hebert and lives in Lacombe, and Viola lives in Edmonton and is married to Clem Giroux.

We continued living on rented land until after the death of my father in 1934. My mother bought the NW 1/4 of section 3-80-20-W5th from Angus McIntyre for $300. We built on this land, and it was our home for many years. When we built the log house, we hired Mr. Hanusz from Rosedale to dovetail the logs, hew the floor joists and ceiling joists, and erect the rafters. For all this work, he charged $27. The shingles were No. 1 cedar and cost $3.75 per square, and, if I remember correctly, the nails were about .05 ¢ per pound. The house is still standing. *(Note: see photo above – page 3)*

Well, we survived the thirties and always had plenty to eat. We would take a 65-bushel load of wheat to the flour mill in Peace River and bring home about a ton of flour, a couple of 100 lb. bags of cream of wheat for porridge, and the bran and shorts that were made in the milling. There was always plenty of wild meat, if one didn't have enough of his own.

Every summer we spent hours picking strawberries, raspberries and saskatoons and, in late

August, made trips to the blueberry patch north of Harmon Valley. On a week-end there would be a couple of hundred people up there. It is almost unbelievable, the tons of blueberries that were picked. We grew a big garden, and the women all exchanged rhubarb recipes.

In those days, no one had much money, so we created our own fun. The Nampa girls had a very good basketball team, and the men and boys had a baseball team. For a few years, there was a league consisting of Rosedale, Judah, Little Prairie, and Nampa. There were a good many dances at the country schools. The men paid .25 ¢ and the women bought a cake or sandwiches.

To add to our cash supply, I spent three years in the bush, hauling and skidding ties. The second winter, I was paid $50 for myself and four horses, and I also supplied a heavy sleigh. Last winter, I skidded thousands of ties at .03 ¢ each. If one worked really hard you could make six or seven dollars a day, and that seemed like a lot of money in those days.

I felt I had a good start that spring and could afford to get married in the fall, so the former Grace Brown and I started making plans.

<u>Note from Dennis:</u>

What Dad failed to mention in his write-up is that from approximately 1951 to 1971, he spent most of the winters working in northern oil camps as a mechanic. Although he wasn't a certified mechanic, he was a pretty good "self-taught" mechanic and jack of all trades and was well thought of and well sought after each fall by various oil companies. Most of his oil company days were spent in Northern Alberta, B.C. or the Northwest Territories. Some of those years were somewhat lean on the farm, but his winter income made sure we were always well looked after. He would often be gone for a month or sometimes two at a time, which seemed like an eternity to us kids, and we were always happy to see him get home."

Dad passed away in November 2002 and is buried next to his parents in the Nampa cemetery.

MOM'S STORY FROM THE NAMPA HISTORY BOOK - PAGES 900 AND 901

I arrived at Nampa on July 15, 1937, along with my parents, sisters and brothers, some goats, a cow, and all our worldly possessions. My dad, Claude Brown, went to work in Brown's store. We lived a mile south of Nampa in the old Vallance house; later, we moved to the big log house known as the Baloc place, half a mile south of Nampa.

There were bushfires south of Nampa that summer of 1937, and the air was always blue with smoke. My dad and my uncle, Mill Brown, made many trips taking groceries out to the firefighters. That was the year the highway was gravelled.

My great aunt, May Brown, had a little restaurant adjoining Brown's store. The gravel crew had their meals there, and I went to work for Aunt May until school started. I was paid the grand sum of .25 ¢ a day. School was held in the old hall. We also went to church there, and to social evenings and dances.

When the hall burned down in 1938, we finished off the school term in the Catholic Church, which was newly rebuilt. Nampa needed a new hall, so money had to be raised. Some of the financial contributions came from a play we put on, "The Scarecrow Creeps."

This was directed by Mrs. Valdene Dewar, the school teacher. Members of the cast were Norma Own, Ted Owen, Howard Hibbard, Eric Hibbard, Pat Bell, George Talbot, Ruth Gillespie, Mrs. Ab Owen, Jim Owen and Grace Brown. Ted Hibbard took care of sound effects, and Claude Brown did make-up. It was spring break-up when we put on the play at Reno.

We travelled with a team and wagon through mud and water. We left early in the day with our stage props and our lunch. It took all afternoon to set up and be ready to perform that night. Later on, we took the play to Rosedale Hall. I can't remember how much money we made. I think the tickets were fifty cents each. Anyway, it was a lot of fun.

Gordon and I were married on Oct. 3, 1940. We hadn't really set a date; we just decided we would be married as soon as harvest was over. In all the years we farmed after that, there were only two years when harvest was completed that early. Gordon was renting land, but there were no buildings on it, so we lived on the NW 1/4 of 2-82-20-W5th, the "Mott homestead."

The building had been empty all summer, and the mice had taken over the house. I did a lot of screeching and jumping on chairs. When cold weather set in, the bedroom was so cold we closed it off for the winter. That was my first deep-freeze. We kept our meat in there, and it stayed frozen all winter.

Dennis was born in June 1941. That summer, it rained constantly. No one could get any summer-fallowing done. Harvest was a terrible ordeal. Gordon ran the separator on a threshing crew, and they spent more time getting the machine from one field to another than they did threshing. They were always stuck in the mud; the fields were so wet, and the roads were terrible. That fall, the crew had breakfast at 5:00 AM and supper whenever they decided to quit. It was a long, weary season.

In December 1941, we moved to Gordon's mother's place. Cliff had joined the army, and they built a little house in Nampa for their mother and two youngest sisters, who were still at home, Viola and Grace. Later on, Grace joined the Air Force.

Our eldest daughter, Valerie, was born in February 1943, and Lynne was born in June 1945. Those were busy years. Gordon farmed Alex and Cliff's land, besides the land he was renting, and we raised pigs. It was almost impossible to get help; sometimes he worked day and night. Our social life was limited, but we still found time to visit the neighbors.

There were picnics and ball games and berry picking expeditions in the summer. In the winter, there were card parties. There were whist drives at Nampa every Saturday night, and we seldom missed one. We played Military Whist, and the prizes were war savings stamps. We, in the Trowsdale district, decided to do something for the war effort too, so we held whist drives every Friday night in different homes.

Most of us travelled with the team and the sleigh, and we took the children. There were no babysitters available; anybody old enough for that job wanted to go to the whist drive too. The Nampa women's institute was organized in the early forties. We packed a lot of parcels to send overseas, donated to the Red Cross, and raised money to buy dishes, chairs, etc., for the Nampa Community Hall.

After the war, we did a lot of catering, and we had to haul the water and a lot of the necessary equipment from home. Once we put on a pancake supper and even hauled a couple of cook stoves to the hall.

It was a cold, stormy night, so we didn't get much of a crowd, but our husbands and kids were all there, and kept coming back for more. We had advertised "all the pancakes, sausages and eggs you can eat." We worked like dogs, but didn't make any profit.

The W.I. also sponsored and helped with the T.B. X-ray clinics at Nampa and sponsored sewing courses, etc. The W.I. was responsible for starting the Fair at Nampa and the Community Library, and the members served as voluntary help in the library for years.

To get back to the McConnells'...in July 1945, we finally bought our own farm, the SE 1/4 of 5-82-20-W5th. We bought it from Olie Gronlund when he decided to go back to Manitoba. It was very close to the Trowsdale school, which we thought would be a real asset, but by the time our children were ready for school, it had gone the way of all the little country schools, and the school bus took the Trowsdale district children to Nampa.

We didn't get our house built until the summer of 1948. It was far from finished when we moved in, but we had lots of room. In March 1951, our youngest son, Gavin, was born.

The Farm Kid And The Flying Bank

By the time he started school, six kids boarded the bus from our place. Chrissie and Dorothy Hogbin stayed with us to attend school at Nampa, as the school at Harmon Valley was being phased out. The last year they were there, Jackie Hogbin started school, so then there were seven. Dennis, Valerie, and Chrissie were going to High School in Peace River by that time, and had to walk two miles to the highway to catch the bus to Peace River. There was quite a commotion getting everyone away on cold winter mornings. We left Nampa in 1972. The children were all grown up and gone, and we had an opportunity to take on a job in Red Deer.

We decided to try it for a year; eight years later, we're still here. We sold the farm in 1973 to Tony and Carol Mayowski. We have a lot of good memories of those many years spent at Nampa, and we are glad we raised our children there. We remember the farmers' Picnic days, the school concerts, the fair, the W.I., Home and School, and Church picnics, the ball games and dances, and especially the wonderful friends and neighbors, who were always ready to help in time of trouble, and shared our good times too.

<u>Note from Dennis</u>:

Mom was born in Burdett, Alberta, spent some of her early years in Calgary, Alberta, where her dad was a bread delivery man (I remember her telling us they got all the "day old" bread they could eat). They then spent some years in the Rimbey, Alberta area before moving to the Peace River country - where mom's story starts. She wrote this for the Nampa area history book published about 1980. Mom died in December 1992 and her ashes are buried in her little sister Neva's grave located on the old Brown family plot (about 2 miles West of the Last West hall) which is about 15 miles west of Rimbey. Her Grandpa and Grandpa Huff are also buried there.

Mom and Dad managed a 100 unit Town house project in Red Deer until about 1981 when they retired and built a nice retirement home in Red Deer. About a year after mom died, Dad sold the house and returned to Peace River to live at "Heritage Towers")

Mom and Dad with their Grandchildren at their 50th. Wedding Anniversary – Oct. 3, 1991.

Back Row L to R: Vail, Thuyen, Bethany, Jean, Jill, Shannon, Lory, Tai, and Shawn.

Seated: Laine, Mathew, Dad, Mom holding Mary Rose, Megan, and Ryan holding Katie.

(Thuyen and Tai are brother and sister, refugees from Vietnam who Val & Keith took in. Val's kids are Bethany, Shannon, and Shawn. Lynne's kids are Vail, Laine, and Megan. Ours are Jean, Jill and Lory; Gavin's kids are Ryan, Mathew, Katie, & Mary Rose.)

APPENDIX – CONNECTING THE DOTS

The McConnell side of my Family:

My Dad had eight siblings who survived childhood, and, in order of age, they were Irene, Gordon (Dad), Pearl, Alex, Mary, Cliff, Gladys, Grace, & Viola. They had at least one sibling who died very young...Aunt Mary told me once of their little sister dying of Scarlet Fever at about 4 or 5 years of age. She remembered that the family was quarantined, and when the little sister died, a wooden box (coffin) was pushed through one of the windows; she was laid in the coffin, and pushed back out the window to avoid close contact with those taking her for burial.

My Dad's older sister, Irene, married Ryerson Hodgins before the McConnell family left Saskatchewan in 1928, and they had two children who were, of course, my cousins. They lived at Davidson, Saskatchewan, so we seldom saw them. We made a big family trip to Saskatchewan to visit them when I was 8, by which time Wes was about 20 and Doris about 18, so both were almost a generation older than me. Wes died of a heart attack when he was relatively young...under fifty, I think. Doris married a farmer, Carmen McNabb. Carmen died in about 2010, and Doris passed away in 2020.

Before we left on the trip to Saskatchewan, my Dad had contacted a niece in Acme, Alberta. We picked her up and took her to Saskatchewan with us.

She was born to Dad's sister Pearl, who died in childbirth, and Doreen was adopted by the Pearson family of Acme. She was about the same age as Doris and continued to live in Acme, and we visited her a couple of times after we moved to Carstairs. Here was a cousin who I didn't know existed until I was 8 and she was 18 *(Doreen passed away in the summer of 2021 at age 91), leaving me as the oldest survivor of some 30 cousins on the McConnell side.*

This photo was taken in Saskatchewan when we were 4, 6, and 8. I believe we were standing on the flat rock, which served as the front step for the home dad was raised in near Girvin, SK.

My Uncle Alex McConnell married Mildred Fletcher, an English War Bride, while overseas. They had a son, Ian, who was born in England. After they arrived in Canada, his sister Sheena was born... a wonderful person, who now lives in Maple Ridge, B.C. Uncle Alex farmed about a half mile north of our home, so Ian and I made many a trip back and forth. The dirt road between our places was loaded with Saskatoon bushes, and we spent many an hour along that road filling our pails. I was like a big brother to Ian. I think Aunt Millie was always a bit leery about letting Ian tag along with me.... she was a very protective mom, and I was a little on the daring side at times.

I started driving our little Ford tractor by the time I was about 9 or 10, but I don't know if Ian ever did drive a tractor...but he loved going along with me...sometimes pulling a stone boat with barrels to their dugout to get water for the cows. Unfortunately, Ian committed suicide in 1985 at the age of 42 while living on the West Coast.

My dad's sister, Mary, married Jim Owen, who just happened to also be my mom's cousin. (Uncle Jim's sister by adoption was Doris, who was my Grade One teacher...and I will talk about her later). As already mentioned, they lived along the river, not far from Nampa. The oldest, Buddy, was two years younger than me (I didn't know until many years later that his name was actually "James").

His brother Glen was the same age as Lynne (1 day older, actually), and their sister Judy was born in 1951 (I think 10 days after Gavin). One day, before the boys were of Junior High age, the family sold out and moved to a farm at Bluesky, Alberta. They were Seven Day Adventist's and wanted to be among a group of "their own". I felt like they were betraying the family at the time, and many years were lost where we could have done more things together. However, we didn't lose touch and made more than one family trip to Bluesky to see them. Unfortunately, Buddy died of cancer at around 52 years of age while living in Ponoka, Alberta, and some years later, Glen died by his own hand.

Uncle Cliff remained a bachelor all his life. He passed away in 2010 at the age of 90.

The Talbot family consisted of Uncle George, who married my dad's sister, Gladys. Edwin was the eldest, then Gail, Neil, Barry, and Danny, and, in later years, they adopted Corry and Colleen. I had left home by this time, so I never got to know them very well. I have noted a bit about the Talbots in Chapter 2 above.

Then there were the Heberts, who lived just down the road from the Talbots (Uncle Fred married Dad's sister, Grace). I was 8 or 10 years old before they started their family, so I was not as close to those cousins...Darlene, the twins Kerry and Karen, Ellen, and the baby Brian, whom I never really got to know.

And there were the Days. My dad's youngest sister, Viola, married Riley Day and they had several children...Lorne, Wayne, Corinne, Donna, Debbie, Darrel, and Mark.

They lived in Edmonton, so we didn't see them very often, although Peggy and I saw a lot of Lorne and his wife, Bonnie, when we lived in Edmonton. Uncle Riley died very young while undergoing heart surgery (in his early 40's, I think). A number of years later, Aunt Viola married Clem Giroux, and they had another daughter, Rhonda. Clem and Aunt Viola both passed away several years ago.

I was posted in Edmonton from sometime in 1964 until sometime in 1966. During those years, we spent a lot of time with Lorne and Bonnie, who had a daughter, Laura, shortly after our Jeannie was born. Bonnie passed away at about 42 years of age from Lung Cancer while they were living in Whitecourt, Alberta. I believe Lorne has remarried and lives near Wildwood, Alberta, although I have not seen or heard from him for many years. (Mark and Corinne both passed away in 2024 or 2025.)

The Brown side Cousins:

Mom had two sisters and four brothers who survived childhood, so we had lots of cousins on that side of the family as well, although none of them lived close to us.

Mom's older sister, Hilda, was married to Alf Bird, and their children were Marvin, Neva, and Alfred. Marvin is about 3 years older than me, Alfred about Lynne's age, and Neva in the middle. Uncle Alf was the hospital Administrator in Lacombe, Alberta, and every few years, we made the long trip south to visit them.

Lacombe was a big place to me, and I enjoyed tagging along with Marv and his friends as they went "up town"...by themselves no less...now this was living like I hadn't known on the farm and I was suitably impressed. Marv and his wife Bev live in Stony Plain, Alberta, Neva is widowed and lives on the West Coast, and Alfred and his second wife live in Edmonton.

Alfred's first wife, Shirley, was in her last year of architecture at the University of Calgary when she died of a brain aneurysm at about 42 years of age. While still in university, she helped Val design the new home that she and Keith had built in Westlock, where Keith practiced dentistry

Mom was the second child, and her sister Viola (always known as "Vee") was the third oldest. She and her husband, Jack Schlenker, had two children, my cousins Velma (about Val's age) and Duane (about Lynne's age). Velma and Duane both live on acreages just west of Edmonton. Aunt Vee divorced and was later widowed, and passed away around 2010.

The eldest son, Rex, spent many of his younger years working in the coal mines at Nordegg and Alexo in Western Alberta. He married Kay Astleford, and they had 5 children who were raised on a farm in the Sangudo area. In order...and all younger than me were Gene, Melvin, Colleen, Sherry, and Denise. Uncle Rex died in 2010 at 83 when he decided that 10 years of Dialysis was enough. Aunt Kay was not in good health and passed away about a year later.

Wayne married Leone Long, and they had three children, Dell, Jeff, and Laurel. Dell inherited all the musical talent (and more) of his uncle Al Brown. Dell & Uncle Al did a lot of jamming together, and played a lot of dances. My cousin Colleen (see above paragraph) is a great singer and usually worked the dances with them, and with Jeff accompanying them on base. Uncle Wayne died of a heart attack in 1991 at the age of 61, and Leone passed away in the early 2000's, as best I can remember.

Uncle Jay married Christine Hogbin, and they had two daughters, Wendy & Corrine, both of whom are around the ages of *my* kids. Jay was only about 5 years older than me, and he met Chrissie while staying at our place on the farm while working in the area. Chrissie and her sister were billeted at our place for several years, as the school bus did not go near their place in Harmon Valley.

Their dad would pick them up on Friday night and bring them back on Sunday night. They were virtually like sisters to us. Mom and Dad received a few dollars (I think $20/month per kid) from the School Board for their room and board. "Aunty Chrissy," as we like to call her, is the same age as my sister Val. Uncle Jay died in 2000 at around 65 years of age due to heart problems.

Mom's youngest brother is Allen, the aforementioned fiddle champ and musician. He married Lorraine Winkelman, and they had four children, all a fair bit younger than me...Darla, Sheila, Russell, and Lorne. Al & Lorraine divorced many years ago. She died around 2000, and Al passed away at Wabumun, Alberta, in about 2021.

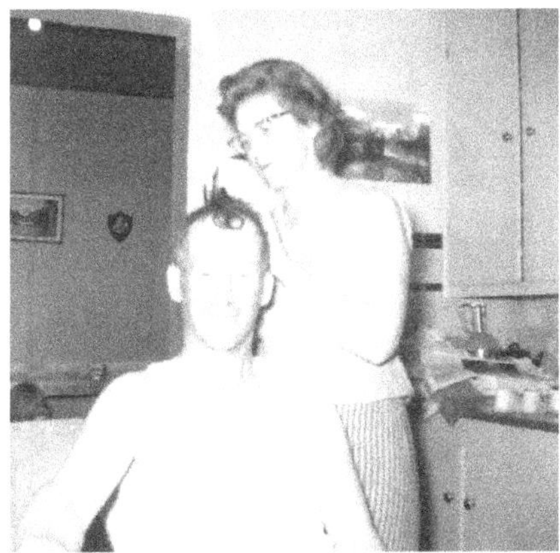

We always liked this photo. I think Peggy or I took this at the farm when we were there for a weekend or a holiday when our kids were small (likely around 1968). Mom had just finished washing Dad's hair and was having fun making it "pretty." Dad just sat there and let her have her fun.

An Update on us:

Peggy has arthritis which can be painful at times, and uncomfortable all the time. As I write this (March 3, 2026) Peggy found out today that she has breast cancer (for the second time) and has an appointment in a few days to review her treatment(s) going forward.

I am dealing with diabetes and cancer but not in any discomfort at all and, with good medical support, seem to be keeping those things in check for now. In January I paid my golf membership for the coming season so hope to be swinging away this summer.

www.ingramcontent.com/pod-product-compliance
Lightning Source LLC
Chambersburg PA
CBHW051239050726
47594CB00001B/235